THE ULTIMATE COACH

CONCENTRATED

THE ULTIMATE COACH

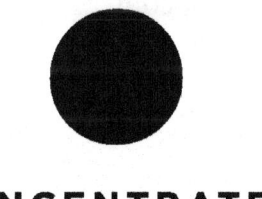

CONCENTRATED

AMY HARDISON

The Ultimate Coach—Concentrated

Copyright © 2024 by Amy Hardison

Zeebroff Books
Mesa, Arizona

Website: theultimatecoach.com

Editing and interior layout: Chris Nelson
Cover design: Angela Hardison

ISBN: 979-8-9851461-5-8

Library of Congress Control Number: 2024908951

First Edition

Dedication

To our grandchildren:

Delaney, Roman, Everest, Enzo

Margo, Ira, Dot

Jonah, Lincoln, and Isaac

A Note from the Author

Amy Hardison

On April 12, 2023, Ranjan Kumar Varanasi in Vizag, India, picked up a phone message. He recognized the voice. He had had many calls with Steve Hardison over the last year as he created and organized The Ultimate Event in Mumbai, India. His experience with Steve prepared him for a big request.

"Hi Ranjan. This is Steve Hardison. There's a thirteen-year-old boy in India named Sasi who called me this morning. He asked me to explain *Being* to him. He would like to read *The Ultimate Coach,* but he doesn't understand English very well. He asked if there was someone who could help him. Ranjan, my request is that we help this young man. Give me a call when you have a minute."

Ranjan texted, "Will definitely help. Will call in a few minutes."

The next day, Ranjan sent Steve an update: "Hi Steve. I spoke with Sasi. He wants me to take him through the entire book word by word. I am going to do that for him. It is going to be fantastic. I don't know what will happen, but I know miracles will come from this.

Thank you so much for this opportunity."

That conversation was the catalyst for this book. It is not a new book. It is *The Ultimate Coach* at its most essential. It is especially appropriate for teens and young adults, but there are plenty of adults who will favor this trimmed-down version.

Those familiar with *The Ultimate Coach* may notice there are no vignettes. Some chapters have been set aside. All chapters are shorter. It weighs in at half the length of the original. These adjustments create a different experience for the reader. It is like drinking orange juice that has been reconstituted with half the amount of water called for.

The Ultimate Coach has been warmly received around the world. We have received numerous emails, texts, and messages from people, thanking us for the difference *The Ultimate Coach* has made in their lives. People have created Ultimate Events, initiated translations, and hosted book-reading Zoom calls. I have been moved and delighted. I believe this book has the same power and punch. It is *The Ultimate Coach Concentrated.*

Sasi and Ranjan, this is for you.

Table of Contents

—⟶〰⟵—

Part One: The Life

Part Two: The Ultimate Coach

Part Three: Steve Hardison—the Man

———⌘———

Before You Begin

Steve Hardison

Note: Thank you for reading the back cover and the first two pages each time before you read this book.

This isn't an ordinary book. It's not simply a biography. It's not a self-help book. It's not a literary classic. It's definitely not a book about how to coach. In fact, it's not a book about *doing* anything.

It's a book about being.

And it's a book about *you*.

To access *this* book, read the back cover and these first two pages **each time** you pick up the book and begin reading. Ask yourself these questions:

> Who would I need to be to know that my life makes a huge difference in this world?

Who would I need to be to know that life is a time to learn, explore, and discover what I love?

Who would I need to be to feel comfortable in my own skin?

Who would I need to be to make and keep promises?

Who would I need to be to show appreciation to others?

Who would I need to be to listen carefully as others speak?

Who would I need to be to realize how talented I am?

Who would I need to be to know I have an extraordinary ability to accomplish whatever I desire?

Who would I need to be to live the most extraordinary life I can live?

Who would I need to be to be fully in love with myself and my life?

Who would I need to be to improve my relationships with the most important people in my life?

Who would I need to be to love and serve others passionately?

Who would I need to be to read *The Ultimate Coach* and have a personal breakthrough in being wonderful me?

The best part about *this* book—this book about *you*—is that it is endless. The story goes on. And it's written by your being.

Loving you. Be Blessed. Be you.
Steve Hardison

P.S. Remember, every time you reread this book, please read the back cover and the first two pages before you begin! If you do this, your experience of this book will be totally different.

SFH/kab

Chapter 1

Enigma

S teve hadn't seen it coming. All he saw was some guy flirting with his girl as they walked down the hall of Clearfield High. When his rage was ignited, Steve didn't see clearly. He missed—or didn't care—that his rival was four inches taller and weighed thirty pounds more. Steve charged at his challenger. "You wanna fight?" he thundered, throwing his fists into fighting position.

Steve took a pounding uppercut to his jaw. He was covered with blood. His tongue would need twenty stitches. His rival hadn't even messed up his own hair.

"Had enough?" Steve roared.

Who says that when he is clearly the loser of a skirmish?

Someone who has swagger. Someone who has something to prove to the world. Someone who is an enigma.

Someone who has a story worth telling.

Part One

The Life

Chapter 2

Roots

Every Sunday Roy Hardison walked three miles to the local church, but not because he wanted to. That is what you did when you grew up in the 1930s in Adairville, Kentucky, and your parents were God-fearing Baptists. Roy fit better with the other Hardisons, the ones known for hard living. Why was he born to the only Hardison brother who was pious?

That wasn't the only thing that galled Roy. His family was dirt poor. Worse, his parents were illiterate. They couldn't even cash their own checks on payday. Plenty of people volunteered to help them, skimming some off the top for their efforts. It was humiliating. He couldn't wait to get out.

Sixteen hundred miles away, Maurine Forbes checked her watch. 9:55 p.m. She wasn't going to make it. She should probably hurry. She slowed down. Who has a 10:00 p.m. curfew when you are eighteen? Her parents had too many rules. *So* overkill. Besides, what was going to happen in Clearfield, a small town in northern Utah, right in the heart of conservative Mormondom? That was the problem. *Nothing* happened in Clearfield. Her parents were strict. Her community was cloying. She couldn't wait to get out.

Roy's ticket out was the air force. He became a paratrooper and was sent to Hill Air Force Base in Clearfield, Utah. On June 9, 1945, Maurine picked him up when he was hitchhiking near the base. He was handsome, slender, and tall—just over 6'4". He was smooth—so smooth Maurine wondered for a moment if he might be a player. Surely not. He was just exciting and fun. Sure, he could talk the birds out of the trees, but there was something beneath the charm that spoke to her, deep in her core, something she had never felt before. Maybe she had just met the love of her life.

Within a year, they eloped.

Ten years later, Maurine sat at her kitchen table in Bitburg, Germany,

Roy Hardison

She stared at her coffee. She didn't realize it was cold.

She knew her marriage was troubled. The more Roy drank, the more troubled it was. But last night left "troubled" in the dust. Her marriage was officially a train wreck.

Maurine had needed a night out. She'd been looking forward to dinner at her favorite restaurant with Roy, a brief respite from the rigors of mothering four young children. Plus, their good friends, Kathy and John, were joining them. Maurine and Kathy were close.

Maurine had put on her favorite dress and taken extra care with her make up, at least as much as was possible with Phil crying for his bottle, Jayme and Teresa bickering about something, and Rob . . . Where was Rob? . . . Oh yes. Out exploring with his friends—sons of other Air Force personnel.

She gave the babysitter her final instructions and then she and Roy were off.

They had just finished dinner with Kathy and John when Roy said, "We have something to tell you."

"We do?" thought Maurine.

Roy grabbed Kathy's hand. "Kathy and I are in love. We want to spend the rest of our lives together."

Maurine's jaw dropped. She looked around the table. John didn't look stunned. Was she the only one who didn't know? John was even smiling. Maybe not smiling exactly. His smile was stiff, like it was painted on.

Kathy pulled her hand away from Roy's. She spoke so softly Maurine could barely hear her.

"Roy, I've changed my mind. I'm staying with John."

Roy stared at her. Then he sized up John.

Roy slowly turned to Maurine and said, "Well, I guess I'll stay with you."

Maurine and Roy (center), and friends

Maurine poured her coffee down the sink and grabbed a pencil and paper. On the left side of the page, she listed all the reasons she should leave Roy. There were many. He had a bad temper—but so did she. She crossed that one off. No one's perfect.

Roy gambled a lot. Poker was his favorite. Too often, his gaming left them scrambling to meet their monthly expenses.

He drank too much.

They fought frequently.

He was the life of the party. At first, she loved that about him. When he was with a group of people, he was animated. He charmed the group with his stories. Some of them even had a kernel of truth. He flirted with the women. He made sure the men were impressed.

It used to be intoxicating, but now she saw the ugly underbelly: he *had* to be the life of the party. He bought steak dinners and rounds of drinks for his friends while Maurine barely had enough money to put food on the table. He was addicted to proving he was not a yokel from the backwoods of Kentucky.

On the right side of the paper she listed the reasons she should stay in her dysfunctional marriage. There was only one: she was pregnant.

On August 14, 1955, Steven Forbes Hardison barged into the world. At 11.5 pounds, he was the biggest baby yet born in the American military hospital in Bitburg, Germany. Little did he know that he was joining a family that was barely hanging together with baling wire and bubble gum.

Roy

As the youngest Hardison, Steve didn't get a lot of his father's attention. That was not a bad thing. Rob, the eldest, got a *lot* of it—and he had peptic ulcers by the time he was twelve.

It's not that Roy didn't love his children; rather, he had an unseemly way of showing it. Roy wanted to pass on his love of baseball to Rob, so he started playing catch with Rob when Rob was two. Their game consisted of throwing the ball *at* Rob, hard, and expecting Rob to catch it. He taught Rob to swim by throwing him into a river in Germany and walking away. Sink or swim. The closest thing Roy ever got to saying "I love you" to Rob was saying to another adult, "That's my boy. See how big he is."

Roy was fun-loving, but with an edge. He put crumbled cornflakes between the sheets of the kids' beds. If the kids were

Steve (left), Phil (right), Rob (center), about 1963

eating ice cream cones, he would smash the ice cream into their faces as they brought the cone up for a lick. He laced Oreos with tabasco sauce.

These were the things he did when he was having fun. Things got worse when he was drinking.

Civilian life

Maurine had moved her family a lot—to Idaho, Colorado, Florida, Texas, France, Germany, and Spain. That's what military families did. But this move was different. It felt like they were slinking away in the middle of the night—which they kind of were. Roy was under military investigation for writing bad checks. If

10

convicted, he would be dishonorably discharged from the Air Force. That would ruin their future. It was better to resign—especially since he *had* written the bad checks. And so, the family headed to Gary, Indiana.

Civilian life didn't go well. Roy was good at getting jobs, but for some reason they never lasted long. His drinking escalated. Homelife became a minefield. Lately, it had been hard to find a piece of ground that didn't detonate. One evening during dinner, Roy launched a bowl of mashed potatoes across the room, potatoes flying everywhere. Roy had lost it because the kids had been too loud.

The most traumatic event of Steve's young life occurred late one night when Roy and Maurine were arguing. Roy was drunk. Maurine was needling him. All five kids were in the house, lying petrified in their beds.

"Stop, mom, just stop," whispered Teresa. "You know dad hates it when you say that."

Maurine didn't stop.

The kids heard a slap and a clatter. Something shattered. Maurine said something, but her words were muffled, deprived of air. Suddenly, a gasp and a cry, "Rob, help me! Rob!"

"If you get out of bed," yelled Roy, "I'll kill you."

No one moved.

Clearfield

Ellen Forbes fretted. Her daughter was in trouble. She was sure of it. Ellen and J. P., Maurine's parents, asked their son Myron to go to Indiana to check on Maurine. Myron feared flying, but he knew his parents wouldn't have asked if things weren't serious. He would do it for Maurine.

When Myron got to Maurine's house, the kids were home alone. Maurine was working at a bar, and Roy had been missing for a week, presumably on one of his benders. Myron reported back to Ellen and J.P. They scraped together the money for six train tickets to Ogden. Maurine and the kids fled before Roy returned.

Ellen and J. P. had almost finished building a house next to their current one. When Maurine arrived with Rob (13), Jayme (11), Teresa (9), Phil (6) and Steve (5), Ellen and J.P. moved into the new house and gave Maurine their old one instead of selling or renting it. Maurine was back home, under the watchful eyes of her parents, in the small town where she had grown up. What a relief.

Ellen and J. P. were sixty-eight and seventy-three when Maurine moved in next door. They were still running their small farm, eleven acres just west of the railroad tracks. They didn't have the time or energy to raise a second family. But they were there for emergencies.

Steve thought having nothing to eat constituted an emergency. Of course, he could always grab the industrial-sized peanut butter they got from the church's welfare center. But how can you eat a peanut butter and jelly sandwich without milk? Their milk came from grandpa's cows and too often had cow hair floating in it. Who could drink that? When he got really hungry, Steve called Grandma Forbes and asked if he could come over and eat.

Ellen always said, "Steve, you know we only have enough for J.P. and me." Once they hung up, Steve would count to twenty. The phone would always ring before he finished counting. "Steve, come on over," said Ellen. "I'll find you something to eat."

There were other emergencies. There were bound to be. Maurine was never at home. She was waitressing full-time and going to school. Sometimes weeks went by without the kids seeing their mom. Rob and Jayme were in charge of the younger kids, but they weren't home much more than their mom. Rob worked as a busboy at the Officer's Club at Hill Air Force Base from 6:00 p.m. to midnight and Jayme worked at Rusty's Drive-in from 5:00 pm to 1:00 am. Teresa, age twelve, was in charge of the house and tried to keep an eye on her brothers.

With little adult supervision, home sometimes felt a little like *Lord of the Flies* or *Survivor*. It had its perks: Steve explored the farms, the culverts, and the town. No one was restraining his curiosity or his propensity for mischief. No adult was hovering. No parent was pushing compliance. He had ample space to be himself.

What it didn't feel like was family, a place of belonging. As far as Steve was concerned, they were a group of lone wolves living in the same house. There were few family dinners and no family vacations. Steve came home from school to an empty house. He played sports with no one in the stands cheering him on. If he was sick, he was at home all by himself. When he had questions, there was no one around to ask.

The worst time to be alone was night. Sometimes he called Grandma Ellen and asked if he could come over. She normally said yes, but Steve was terrified of the dark, a fear that lasted until he was fifteen. To get to Grandma Ellen's, Steve had to cross the sector of terror between his back porch and his grandma's back door. It wasn't far, but it felt like three miles.

Steve's fears weren't groundless. Sketchy-looking men often walked by Steve's house after working at the nearby Job Corp, a job-training program for at-risk young adults. Late one night, Steve was awakened by the scuff of his window sliding open and a burst of winter cold. Steve opened his eyes to see a man climbing through his window.

Steve closed his eyes and feigned sleep. *Mom, help!* Steve thought. *Wake up. Please, wake up.*

The intruder crept closer. Steve tried to still his breathing. He willed his body to quit trembling. He silently screamed, *Mom. . . Rob. . . God. . . Anyone. Make him go away!*

The prowler was close enough for Steve to smell cigarettes on his breath. Suddenly, Maurine shrieked, "Rob, get your gun. Someone's in the house." The prowler bolted out the window. Good thing, because they didn't have a gun.

But bluster wouldn't keep the real threat away. Even though they were divorced, Roy was in the wings. He was *always* in the wings. From time to time he would phone, just so Maurine wouldn't forget. "They are my kids, you know. You can't keep them away from me. Even if you tried, I could come and take them when you aren't home. Just like you did to me."

Maurine lived in fear—but it turned out she didn't need to. Roy found a new woman to love. It was inconvenient that this other woman was already married, but that wasn't insurmountable. Beatrice left her husband and children and married Roy. They had a son together. Roy named him Rob, again. Maybe he wanted a do-over.

Roy only showed up in Clearfield once. Steve was young, about five. They were in the back yard of the house J.P. and Ellen had given them, the house that would be Steve's home for the next fourteen years. As Roy lifted Steve onto the back porch, Steve looked up and saw the Rocky Mountains that flanked the valley. "Dad, will you take me to those mountains?"

Roy ruffled Steve's hair. "Of course, son. That would be fun. You can count on it."

Steve never saw his father again.

Family picture: Steve (left), Jayme, Rob, Teresa, Phil, about 1962

Chapter 3

Growing Up

S teve raised his hand. Mrs. Gailey didn't call on him. He waved his arm. He waved both arms. He bounced in his seat. Finally, his question erupted. "Mrs. Gailey, how far is it to the moon?"

"Steve, we are talking about the pilgrims."

Yes, but Steve was thinking about space. He had been ever since his grandpa pointed out the Big Dipper the previous night. Didn't Mrs. Gailey know how hard it was to keep all those questions bottled up inside? Didn't she know how exhausting it was sitting at a desk for seven hours a day like a trussed-up turkey?

Maybe she did know. She always gave him an extra hug. Mr. Fernelius didn't. He said things like, "Put a rag in that kid's mouth." The first time Mr. Fernelius said that, Steve felt like he had been sucker punched.

Most adults really liked Steve, except when they didn't. He

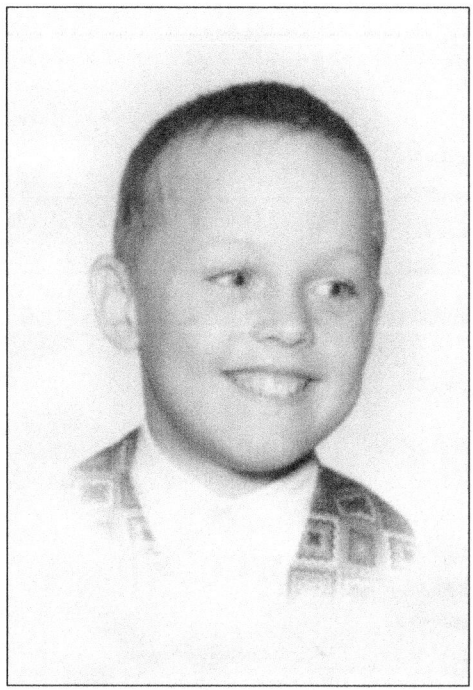

Steve, 1962

rubbed some the wrong way. Perhaps he had too much confidence. Or perhaps he was just too much. He never could figure out why some teachers shaved yards off his mark when he threw the softball and added seconds to his time when he ran the fifty-yard dash when testing for the Presidential Fitness Award in P.E. He *knew* he ran faster and threw the ball further than anyone in his grade. He had told his teachers so. He had told his classmates. Why would they want to knock him down a peg? He saw it in their faces. He felt it. But it made no sense to him.

Steve hated when things didn't make sense. Sometimes his homework didn't make sense. At times like these, frustration surged through his body. He felt like the Incredible Hulk. Something took over. It transformed him, and he *became* rage. Sometimes he broke things. Sometimes he threw things. Sometimes he punched holes in the walls. Why didn't his mom see he needed someone to hold him, to love him, to tell him everything would be okay? But his mom was either absent or moralizing. When he was the most broken, she walked away, leaving him in the rubble.

Maurine completed a bachelor's degree in business administration and secured a job as an executive housekeeper for the Rodeway Inn in Salt Lake City. She was a natural leader. She got results and her people loved her. But that didn't translate into more time at home. Money was still tight. It would always be tight. That's the way it was in 1964 if you were a single mother working in a world that favored men.

"Mom," said Steve one evening. "Now that I'm ten, I can play Pop Warner football. I really, *really* want to play. Dennis is playing. So is Gene Johnson. And Blake Murdock. All my friends are playing. Here is the paperwork. All I need is twenty dollars for the uniform."

Maurine looked up from the table where she sat paying bills. "Steve, I don't have enough money for the doctor's bill for your stitches last month. I don't have enough money for our utilities. A football uniform is way down the list. I'm sorry."

"Yeah, I know." Steve turned away, disappointed but not surprised. It had been worth a try. Steve knew there was always a way to get what you wanted. He started selling magazine subscriptions door-to-door. He got paid for talking. Pretty sweet. He suited up with his Pop Warner team a few months later.

Brrrring. Brrrring.

Maurine held her breath when the phone rang. She crossed her fingers and picked it up. "Yes?"

"Is this Steve Hardison's mom?"

"Yes."

"You need to get to the donut shop, quick. There's been an accident."

Within minutes, Maurine stood at the door of the donut shop— or at least where the door used to be. Now there was just jagged glass and blood. Steve's bicycle lay in the debris. She peered in. Steve was sitting on the counter, his hand wrapped in a bloody towel.

He's alive, she thought. Whew.

On their way to the hospital to stitch up his wounds, Maurine asked Steve what happened.

"I wanted to throw my bike into a skid. I guess I was going too fast, and I miscalculated. Sorry."

"And just why did you want to put your bicycle into a skid?"

Steve looked a little sheepish. "There was this cute girl watching."

Maurine wasn't sure if she was more relieved or irritated. Mostly she wondered, "How am I going to pay for this?" Steve's injuries would eventually fill a medical chart. There were concussions (in the plural), knocking out his front teeth in a basketball game, nearly knocking out his bottom teeth when he fell water skiing and the ski hit his mouth. The dentist had to wire his teeth back into their sockets and Steve had to eat baby food for three months. There were broken bones and torn ligaments.

It's not that Steve was clumsy or unlucky. Rather, he was intense. He was adventurous. When a thought took him, he went with it. Why let a little thing like common sense get in the way?

Maurine thought it was important that her children get religion. She just didn't want to be the one to do it. Good thing Ellen and J.P. wanted her kids to go to church with them. J.P. loved to go to the pulpit on the first Sunday of each month when members of the congregation shared their testimonies. Sometimes he would go off and start talking about how far away the stars were and where heaven is. Steve noticed that the bishop of his congregation started fidgeting the longer J.P. talked. If J.P. talked for too long, the bishop asked him to sit down. They didn't do that for anyone else. Those were Steve's favorite Sundays.

Well, his second favorite. His favorite was when Maurine dropped him off at church. Then, as soon as her car was out of sight, he would make a beeline for the nearby Chevron station and shinny up a tree. For the next hour, Steve watched cars go by and daydreamed. That was the way he liked his religion.

Steve didn't restrict his daydreaming to Sundays. He often made his way to the shed on J.P.'s farm. He would sit there for hours. If the sun was just right, he could see dust particles floating in the sunlight. They looked like the universe. Sometimes he would cry, but mostly he thought. "What's life all about? Why is it like this?" Sometimes he went down the rabbit hole thinking about thinking. "There are thoughts in here. Who's doing that?"

Eighth grade was a banner year. Steve started on the football, basketball, and baseball teams. He was a class officer. He was adored by girls, gregarious, and popular. He was confident. More than confident, he was cocky. But in ninth grade, things started to unravel. By tenth grade at Clearfield High, his inner world was shattered. All his friends' voices had dropped. They were adding muscles and inches to their frames. Steve looked like a little boy. It's a hard thing to hide, especially in the locker room.

One game day after a tough loss against a rival junior high basketball team, Steve's angst came out in tears. His coach, Carl Clayton, approached him. "Hardison, are you upset about the loss?"

"No. It's not that . . . Coach, what if I never grow?"

"You don't need to worry about that," responded Clayton. "You are going to be at least 6'4". I played baseball with your dad at Hill Field. Your body is just like his. You are going to grow."

"You knew my dad? I have never met anyone that knew my dad . . . 6'4"?"

After practice, Steve pedaled home, making it in record time. He was fueled by euphoria.

The Rebel

Steve was playing catcher. He loved that position because he was in every play. Phil was in center field. Phil had a powerful arm. As a ninth grader, he could throw a runner out at home from center field. And for once, they had a spectator. That didn't happen often. The people that mattered most to Steve were always working. But this day, Rob was in the stands, cheering Steve and Phil on. Steve played his best, hoping to impress Rob.

After the game, Rob approached the coach. Steve moved a little closer, hoping to hear what they were saying, hoping for some praise.

"Our dad was great at baseball," Rob said. "He wanted me to play, but . . . I didn't take to it. He would be thrilled to see Steve and Phil out here on the field. They're pretty good, right?"

"Oh, they're great. They have talent. They have drive. I wish all my players understood baseball the way they do. But . . ."

Rob waited for the coach to finish his sentence, but the coach seemed to have changed his mind.

"But what?" prompted Rob.

"Well, that brother of yours, Steve. He'd better watch his mouth. He's a smart ass."

Rob shrugged his shoulders. Steve just grinned.

Not only was Steve a smart ass, he was also a rebel. He questioned authority. He disregarded rules. He liked the thrill of living on the edge. You could blame it on being a teenager, but Steve's defiance was evident in elementary school. When he was in the fourth grade, he learned how to place a rock in the threshold of the cafeteria doorway so the door didn't completely shut. He would come back at night and help himself to all the cookie dough, chocolate milk, and orange juice he wanted. And it was so much more fun when he brought his friends.

At fourteen, Steve and his friends would skip out of church services and hunt through the parking lot for unlocked cars. "Hey, guys. Found one," Steve would yell as he slipped into the driver's seat. His friends surrounded the car while Steve shifted to neutral. "One . . .two. . . three . . . push."

Once they got the car rolling, they pointed it towards the junior high parking lot. It didn't take long until it was parked in an inconspicuous corner. They gave each other high fives and ran to their hiding places.

"What time is it?" asked Dennis.

"Showtime," said Steve, just as the church members started to exit the church.

The responses were predictable: confusion, then panic, then anger. Steve chortled with delight.

Steve had no problems sneaking in or sneaking out, whatever the occasion called for. Like the time he and Larry Belnap went to Salt Lake City for a rock concert and met some girls who were in the city for a church youth conference. The girls invited them up to their hotel room. No problem—until the girls' chaperone started banging on the door. Steve and Larry ended up hanging off the balcony to avoid detection. They were on the twelfth floor.

And there was the time when Steve had to sneak into his own house, don his pajamas, and look slightly sleepy when the police came calling about a group of teenagers pelting cars with apples from a nearby orchard. Funny how the police went straight to the Hardison household.

As he got older, Steve's mischief took a darker turn. He became adept at shoplifting. He steered clear of drugs, but he drank plenty of alcohol. While working at the Rodeway Inn as a linen boy, Steve would pour the leftover alcohol from the mini bottles people left in their rooms into a gallon bottle. When the bottle was full, they had enough for their weekend party.

It had been a while since Steve had sat in the shed on his grandpa's farm. It would always be his refuge, where he sorted out his thoughts. And right now there was so much to sort out. He craved acceptance, but he hated to conform. He loved to be unorthodox, but he hated being judged for it. He was afraid he would never grow. He was anxious about his future.

No one at high school had a clue about his private despair. He was popular. The girls liked him. His social currency was high. But underneath the bravado, the cool, and the charisma, he was lost.

He also had several unresolved issues from his childhood that he had stuffed down inside, down to his toes, so far down he didn't know they were there, so far down they wouldn't see light for another thirteen years. But they were still there, messing with Steve, like radiation.

Chapter 4

Finding God

S teve leaned back in his chair and kicked up his feet. Seminary, the release-time class for religious instruction for Mormon high school students, was sandwiched between English and Biology. It was a nice break. Lorrie Weeks, the cutest blonde in the senior class, sat behind him, combing his hair. If Steve had been a cat, he would have been purring. Half-way between sleep and nirvana, Steve felt someone standing over him. He opened one eye and saw the instructor of his seminary class glaring at him.

"Steve, we need to talk. In the hall. Now."

"Aren't you supposed to be teaching?"

"This is more important," said Brother Fraser.

In the hall, Brother Fraser spoke with a quiet intensity. "Steve, why are you here?"

Steve pointed at the classroom and replied with casual insolence,

"Lorrie . . . And no homework . . . And I want one of those fancy graduation certificates."

"That's not why you come to seminary. You come to seminary to learn about God and Jesus Christ." Looking hard into Steve's eyes, Brother Fraser asked, "Steve, do you believe in God?"

Steve matched Brother Fraser's gaze, eye to eye, force to force. "If there's a God, He hasn't been around my house much."

After a minute, Brother Fraser said, "Steve, instead of coming to class, why don't you go to my office and read the Book of Mormon. Find out for yourself if it's true. Find out if God is real."

Steve considered the invitation. He didn't answer right away. His relationship with The Church of Jesus Christ of Latter-day Saints was complicated.

He pictured his grandparents, faithfully attending church every week. "They love it. They live it," thought Steve. "They are good people. Heck, their grandparents walked half-way across the country in the 1850s just so they could live in Utah with the Latter-day Saints. It kind of feels like they are my people."

"Yeah, but they also kicked me out of the Boy Scout troop, just because I punched that obnoxious kid. Everyone *wanted* to punch him. I hated scouting anyway."

But he *did* love basketball. Steve's face went hot when he thought of Bishop Lyman pulling him off the basketball court right in the middle of the game. "Just because I hadn't attended church often enough." It was humiliating. "I don't know if I want anything to do with them."

A cheeky grin unfurled when Steve thought of the Sunday services he had spent crawling around in the church's rafters, having accessed the attic through a crawlspace he discovered. And when he prepared the Sacrament, he had often used rusty water and pushed the Sacrament cups down extra hard so people had to wrestle them out of the tray, often spilling them. "Maybe they don't want anything to do with me."

Then he thought, "No. They want me. Brother Stoker keeps coming to our house every month to check on us, even when we pretend we aren't home."

Steve's musings were hijacked by the fear that surfaced whenever his waters got too still. "What am I going to do when I graduate?" The post-high school abyss was just around the corner, and it was terrifying. Plus, Steve felt a flicker of something as Brother Fraser spoke to him. Whatever it was, it was worth checking out.

After a few weeks of his personal study hall, Steve noticed a difference. He felt peaceful inside. He was consistently happy. No, not happy, something deeper. Joyful. He looked forward to his study time in Brother Fraser's office. That little office felt sacred, otherworldly. He felt close to God. He cut his hair. He quit drinking. No one made him. No one even suggested it. It just felt like the right thing to do. Instead of hanging out with his friends after school, he went home and continued to study. There was so much to learn. He felt like he was starting a race after all the other runners had already run two laps.

Steve's church leader, Bishop Doug Barrus, noticed. He called Steve in for a visit. After some general chit-chat, he leaned forward and asked, "What are your goals for the future, Steve?"

Future? He had been trying hard to *not* think about the future. Goals? He pictured his mom sitting at the kitchen table with the bills spread out in front of her. Her brow was furrowed, her voice strained. That was when she would tell him he would never be able to buy a new car or own a house. That was a pipe dream for people like them. "Survive. I want to survive—and maybe own a car one day." That is what Steve wanted to say.

When Steve didn't answer, Bishop Barrus moved on. "What are your thoughts about a mission?"

"A mission? You want me to be one of those guys who wears a white shirt, tie, and black name badge? And pedals around on a bicycle for two years? And knocks on doors for two years? And no dating for two years?"

"Just think about it."

"Don't missions cost money?" asked Steve.

"We can talk about that later. For now, just pray about it," said Bishop Barrus. "In the meantime, I have something for you to do. Get a pad of paper and write down all the things you need to repent of."

"All of them? That could take a while . . . How will I remember everything?"

"Ask Heavenly Father to bring the things you need to repent of to your mind. Every time you think of something, write it down."

"I can do that," said Steve. He was excited to do it. It felt like a quest.

When he returned the next week, his list was several legal pages long. "Bet you've never seen a list this long," joked Steve. Bishop Barrus hadn't. He thumbed through the pages. Steve had been thorough.

"What's next?" asked Steve.

"Now, you ask God for forgiveness. You commit to change. And you make restitution."

Immediately, Steve thought about last summer when he drove to the local golf course, to the stand where golfers leave their clubs when they go into the pro shop to get their tee times and golf carts. He had grabbed a couple sets of clubs, thrown them into his trunk, and driven away. At the time, he relished how easy it had been. He kept the owners' name tags as a kind of trophy. He knew what he needed to do. He would call the owners, explain what he had done, apologize, and offer to pay for the clubs.

Stolen golf clubs, pilfered eight-track tapes, and purloined belts—those were the easy things to make right. Some things were more abstract. Some things would be mortifying.

Steve called or visited every person on his list. He repented for every transgression he could recall. The response was consistent. People were not angry; they were moved. It took Steve six months. The process was life-altering.

The next time he met with Bishop Barrus, Steve said, "Bishop, can we talk about that mission?"

Steve walked into the kitchen to make himself a peanut butter and jelly sandwich. Phil was there, searching the fridge for something to eat. When Phil looked up and saw Steve, he fell on his knees, made the sign of the cross, and said, "Forgive me, Padre, for I have sinned."

"Very funny," said Steve. "That's what Catholics say, not Mormons."

"It's all the same to me," replied Phil. "By the way, if I haven't already said it, I think you're crazy for going on a mission. "

"You've said it plenty."

"Well, while you are out there knocking on doors, I'll be dating, working at a job I like, and earning money for my own car. No contest, man."

That was exactly what Steve thought.

Chapter 5

A Man on a Mission

Steve had been checking the mailbox daily. Finally, the oversized, white envelope with the words "The Church of Jesus Christ of Latter-day Saints" in the upper left corner arrived. He didn't wait to gather family or friends. He went straight to Grandma Ellen and together they opened the letter that would chart the next two years of Steve's life. He read the words: "You are hereby called to be a missionary . . . to labour in the England London South Mission. You are scheduled to enter the Mission Home in Salt Lake City on Saturday, 12 October, 1974 . . . We ask that you please send your written acceptance promptly."

Steve's first thought was, "I'm teaching The Beatles. I'm teaching the Queen."

Three months later, Steve flew out of Salt Lake City to the London Heathrow airport. He had no problem leaving behind his old life. Instead of working, dating, and even just kicking back and watching sports on television, he would spend every waking moment with his companion. They would work together, study together, eat together, and live in the same apartment. From morning to night, they would knock on strangers' doors and stop people in the street and tell them they had a message from God. Ideally, they would teach them a set of missionary lessons and the people would then be baptized and join the church. So many members of Steve's faith had assured him this would be one of the greatest experiences of his life.

After one week in England, Steve knelt by his bed to pray before going to sleep. "Dear Heavenly Father . . ." He bit his lip. He swallowed down the sob that was trying to escape. Stiff upper lip and all that stuff. He couldn't let his companion know he ached to see something familiar. He couldn't let him know that he was scared, that he wondered what he was doing on a mission, and that two years seemed like a lifetime.

His companion figured it out. Out of the darkness, Steve heard his companion's voice, "Pray your heart out, elder. Pray your heart out."

Steve soon adjusted to a new country, a new way of life, and new responsibilities. In fact, he thrived. He became known as the missionary who didn't even stop to eat. He learned that eating Weetabix cold cereal three times a day saved a lot of time.

Steve was comfortable talking to strangers. He loved meeting people. He was never at a loss for something clever or fun to say. He was talking the birds out of the trees.

One day, Steve looked around at the town where he was tracting (knocking on doors to find people to teach) and realized that missionaries had been tracting there since 1842. If he wanted someone to listen to him, he had better get creative.

Steve and his companion walked up to the red brick house and knocked on the door. No one answered. Just as they turned to walk away, someone flicked open the mail slot and a female voice said, "We know who you are. We aren't interested."

Steve said, "My name is Elder Hardison, and this is Elder Waite. What is your name?"

"Doreen Crook," she responded.

"Is your husband home? Could we talk to him?" asked Steve.

"I'm ironing his trousers. He's not available. He's in the back room with his trousers down."

"You're telling me that you have a crook in your house with his trousers down and you haven't called the police yet?"

Steve heard someone laughing. "Let them in," Mr. Crook said as he slipped on his pants.

Steve baptized Mr. and Mrs. Crook and their children.

Steve continued to come up with fun, creative ways to speak with people. Sometimes, when they tracted in apartment buildings, Steve would have his companion walk up one flight of stairs. Steve would knock on the door and when someone answered, he would say, "We are here to tell you about a book from heaven." On that cue, his companion would drop a Book of Mormon and it would land in Steve's hands. Every now and again, the book would hit Steve's glasses and knock them off-kilter.

While knocking on doors in the village of Claygate, Steve and his companion met a woman named Julia Burgess. She was open and receptive. Soon, she was baptized.

The night before Steve met Julia, she was sitting on her front porch smoking a cigarette. She was divorced and was raising two young boys. There wasn't enough money for their basic needs. She was exhausted and discouraged. It all seemed like too much. Julia pled, "God, if you are there, you are going to have to tell me. You are going to have to help me. Otherwise, I'm going to end it all." Steve and his companion knocked on her door the next morning. When she answered, they told her they had a message from God.

Two years passed quickly. Steve had promised God he wouldn't waste a minute. He had kept his promise. He had served and loved the people. He had drawn close to God. He didn't even remember the other Steve Hardison, the one who was lost and uncertain. He barely remembered his home and family. The only life that felt real was his mission in England. But now he had to return home.

During his exit interview with his mission president, President Eyre asked Steve about his plans once he got home. President Eyre suggested Harvard. Harvard? Steve hadn't even planned on college until this interview. He was beginning to see that his mission had changed the trajectory of his life in so many ways.

Every day of his mission he had prayed, "God, I'm giving everything I've got. Every day I am teaching people about eternal families. Please, when I get home, help me find someone I can create a loving and eternal family with."

Chapter 6

Meeting Amy

Steve knew nothing about Arizona except that it had cacti and Indians and it was where his mom now lived. She had moved there when he was in England. Steve had no interest in Arizona, but he wanted to see his mom, so he made the thirteen-hour drive to the valley of perpetual sunshine. He never intended to stay long. Before he knew it, he was helping with the missionary preparation class at church, working at Woolco, and living in Arizona.

The missionary prep class was led by Gordon Jennings. Steve and another young man, David Bedford, were asked to help and support Gordon. As Gordon got to know Steve, he saw a man with fierce spiritual conviction, just like Gordon's sister-in-law, Amy Blake. The longer Gordon knew Steve, the more convinced he was that Steve and Amy should meet.

Amy walked into her house one Sunday evening and noticed a note on the kitchen counter. She picked it up. It was from her sister, Melinda. "Amy, Gordon is bringing someone over for you to meet about 8:00. Be there. Look cute." It was 8:05. The doorbell rang. Amy hoped she looked cute enough.

Gordon walked in with two gentlemen. One was the most handsome man Amy had ever seen. He was movie-star good-looking.

The other was Steve Hardison.

Steve had the strangest hairstyle Amy had ever seen. It looked like a yarmulke perched on top of his head. But he was dazzling. He had charm, charisma, and confidence. He *definitely* had confidence. Gordon, Steve, and David visited with Amy and her family for an hour.

As they walked out of the house, Gordon turned to Steve. "What do you think? Do you want her phone number?"

"How old is she? She looks really young."

"She's an old soul," Gordon said. "Here's her number, just in case."

Steve didn't call—not the next day and not the next week. But the following week, Steve picked up the phone and dialed her number. Their phone conversation was interesting enough that Steve asked Amy on a date. She suggested making doughnuts. The date was set for the next evening, February 10, which happened to be Amy's mom's birthday.

Four days later, Steve was passing out Valentine's Day cards. He had bought a dozen and had one left over. Might as well drop it off for Amy. He personalized the card by writing, "Let's play tennis sometime. R.S.V.P." Amy took that as a legit request. She sent him a tennis ball in the mail. Then the magic started.

One date had an extra measure of magic. Steve invited Amy for a bike ride and a picnic. He would bring the food. Amy was puzzled when he showed up empty-handed. Maybe she had misunderstood the lunch part. They jumped on their bikes and off they pedaled. They ended up at the playground of a grade school.

"Have you ever had a peanut butter-honey-and-banana sandwich?" Steve asked.

"No. I have never even heard of it."

"It's delicious," affirmed Steve.

"Hmm." Amy was skeptical.

After a bit, Steve said he was hungry. "I have an idea. I'll go ask someone if they will make us lunch, maybe even peanut butter-honey-and-banana sandwiches."

Before Amy had finished determining if Steve would really ask a stranger to make them lunch, Steve was knocking on the door of a house across the street. A middle-aged woman opened the door. Steve made his request. She stared at him and then said, "Are you serious?" Steve assured her he was. She started to shut the door and then in mid-motion changed her mind. "Are you really serious?" she asked once more.

"Now's the time," Amy thought. "Here is where you say you were just kidding. . . Here. . . Right now. . . "

Steve just nodded.

In about ten minutes, she reappeared with a paper sack. Amy peeked in. There were two sandwiches, two salads, and drinks.

"Now, all we need is a blanket," said Steve.

Steve dragged Amy to the next house. A gruff-looking man opened the door. "Sir, do you have a blanket we could use for a picnic?"

He grunted, handed Steve a blanket that was sitting by the door, and turned away.

The peanut butter-honey-and-banana sandwiches were surprisingly good, but Amy wasn't focused on them. She had a lot to digest. "Does Steve always do stuff like this?"

Low-grade bewilderment escalated to full-blown anxiety when Steve folded up the blanket and started riding in the opposite direction from the man's house.

"Where are you going? We have to take the blanket back," said Amy.

Steve kept pedaling.

"Steve, we need to take the blanket back."

He kept pedaling.

"I'm not joking. We have to take the blanket back to its owner. Really."

Finally, Steve turned his bike around. "I am."

Then Amy got it. This was no casual ride to the park. This date had been carefully planned and executed. It was fair warning that Steve would never be conventional. He would be fun. He would be outrageous. This would be an adventure.

They had just finished watching the Church's semi-annual conference on television. Steve looked at Amy as they sat on the couch in his mom's apartment. He loved how her eyes sparkled, especially when she smiled. When he was with her, he felt safe. He wanted to be with her all the time.

"So, we have two hours before the afternoon session of the conference. Is there anything specific you want to do?" asked Steve.

When Amy said no, Steve suggested studying the scriptures. That is what he had done daily with his companions while on his mission. He had been home from his mission for six months and he missed studying with another person. When Amy opened her bible and Steve saw the notes and markings, evidence of Amy's love for the scriptures, he knew he had found his wife.

There was just one problem. Amy was seventeen. She was still in high school.

Steve and Amy met on January 23, 1977. Their first date was on February 10, 1977. On April 20, 1977, Steve asked Amy to marry him. Amy's mom, Carol Blake, was nervous. Not only was Amy only seventeen, but Steve had just barely rolled into town. He was a sweet talker, but was he as good as he looked?

When Steve asked Amy's father, Kent, for permission to marry Amy, Steve told him that he didn't know how to be a husband or a father. He had seen more divorces than successful marriages in his family. Kent was not ignorant of the risks. However, he saw Steve's potential. He gave his approval.

The next day, Steve drove away. He felt the weight and responsibility of finding a place to live and a way to support his soon-to-be bride. Utah, where he had contacts and opportunities, was definitely the place to do it. He enrolled in Weber State University in Ogden, Utah, found work at Hill Air Force Base, and got licensed to sell real estate.

Throughout that summer, Steve and Amy dated long distance. Once or twice, they saw each other. Sometimes they called each other—but long-distance phone calls were expensive. Mostly they wrote letters, real postal mail that took three or four days to travel between Arizona and Utah. They wrote nearly every day.

At the end of August, Amy moved to Provo, Utah, to attend

Engagement, 1977

Brigham Young University, something that had been arranged before she had met Steve. Now they were only seventy-two miles apart. Steve drove from Clearfield to Provo to see her every weekend until they got married.

Steve and Amy chose December 20, 1977 for their wedding date. They would leave immediately after Amy's last final on December 18 and drive to Arizona. They would arrive the night before the wedding. But there was a snag. At that time, in Arizona you had to have a wedding license at least forty-eight hours before a wedding. The solution was to get their wedding license when they went to Arizona for Thanksgiving. When Steve and Amy went to the county Superior Court's office the day after Thanksgiving, the employee took one look at Amy's birth certificate and said, "I can't give you a marriage license unless a parent signs for her. She is only seventeen."

Chagrinned, they returned to Amy's house and asked Carol to come with them and sign for Amy to get married. It's a good thing Carol had warmed up to Steve and the idea of her daughter getting married so young.

Two weeks later, Amy turned eighteen. Two weeks after that, Steve and Amy got married.

Steve and Amy, 1977

Chapter 7

Newlyweds

Most evenings, Steve and Amy sat at their kitchen table doing their homework. Amy wore her coat and scarf. She had to. There was ice on the inside of the windows. The 700-square-foot, little pink house Steve had purchased from his grandmother was an ideal starter home for them, but it wasn't exactly energy efficient.

They drove a 1971 Duster that sported a huge dent in the front and squawked with right turns. They carried power steering fluid in the trunk for when the screech got too loud. When the heater went out in the car, they didn't have money to fix it. The morning drives to Weber State University were bone-chilling. On occasion, they splurged and went out to eat at Tony's Pizza in Ogden or bought a Cosmos burger at the hamburger joint down the street. Mostly, they spent their nickels and dimes sparingly. But they were in love and happy, most of the time.

Their first house-improvement project was painting their kitchen cabinets. Steve didn't like the way Amy painted. He snapped at her. It was harsh. She was shell-shocked.

Amy thought it was an exception. It wasn't. Steve was easily frustrated. When he was frustrated, he snapped at Amy. She wasn't used to being snapped at. It hurt. She withdrew. Steve got angry. Amy shut down.

Steve wondered why Amy often looked like a deer caught in the headlights.

Amy wondered if this is what all newlyweds went through.

One day, the phone rang. Steve picked up. It was his close friend and former mission companion, Paul Waite. Amy didn't mean to eavesdrop, but their house wasn't that big.

It was a typical conversation—school, work, sports, married life. Then she heard Steve say, "These women, they're extra baggage." She felt like she had been kicked in the stomach, or perhaps a little higher. In the heart.

This wasn't what she had expected.

It took them decades to work out their challenges. They had to dig deep—deep into Steve's past, deep into pain Steve had tried to erase. Amy had to jettison the model of her parents' idyllic marriage and create realistic expectations for her own marriage. The work was rigorous and soul-stretching. At times, the challenges almost won.

Chapter 8

Weber State

Steve stepped into a furniture store in a little strip mall on Main Street in Clearfield. The owner, Jim Barlow, hoped he was a customer. Steve glanced around. He saw four salespeople and no customers. That wasn't promising, but Steve needed a job, something he could do after his morning classes at Weber State.

After introducing himself, Steve said, "Would you like some ideas on how to increase foot traffic?" Jim was interested.

After sharing several ideas, Steve said, "Jim, I would love to come and work for you for thirty days on straight commission. At the end of thirty days, you could decide if you want to keep me."

What was there to lose?

Within two days, Jim knew he wanted to keep Steve. He paid him $4.37 per hour, plus commission. In an exceptional month, Steve brought home $800. In his downtime, Steve could do his homework.

Steve's mind was always whirring, coming up with creative ideas to help the store. He had his mom's business sense and his father's gift of gab. He had been in sales in one way or another since he sold magazine subscriptions door-to-door as a ten-year old.

Not everyone who walked into the store walked out with a purchase. Sometimes, they didn't find what they wanted. Sometimes the price was out of their budget. Steve saw an opportunity. Jim let Steve buy furniture at cost plus ten percent. Steve had been buying things for their house at the employee rate, a little here and a little there. Sometimes, Steve had a piece of furniture at his house that fit the needs of a customer, one who couldn't pay full price at Barlow's. Steve could sell it at a price that was affordable for the customer and profitable for him. Jim agreed.

Later, when Amy was eight-and-a-half months pregnant and couldn't sleep, she got out of bed.

"Where are you going?" Steve asked through a yawn.

"I'm going to rock in the rocking chair. Maybe that will help me fall back asleep."

"You can't," Steve responded. "Remember, I sold it today."

When the time came to pay their obstetrician for delivering their firstborn, Steve worked out a trade in furniture.

Weber State University

Steve and Amy went to school together year-round. Steve majored in business and communications and Amy majored in English. Amy was always excited about what she was learning in her classes. She would talk most of the way home about this short story or that fascinating theme. When she would ask Steve about his classes, he would say, "They were good." This became a pattern that would play out over and over throughout the years. Amy was excited about what she learned. Steve was excited about the people he met.

Steve loved attending Weber State's football and basketball games, and the cost fit right into their budget—free. They rarely missed a game. One crisp, autumn night, Steve and Amy attended a Weber State football game with Amy's sister and brother-in-law, Melinda and Gordon, who had come from Arizona to visit them.

At the end of the first quarter, the announcer's voice came through the speakers. "Listen up, all you Wildcat fans. If you have a star on page twenty-three of your program, you are in luck. You can enter the half-time field goal contest. First prize is $250."

Two hundred and fifty dollars! That was a third of Steve's monthly income—in one night. He hoped he had a star. Steve flipped to page twenty-three.

"Gordon, look. I got a star. This will be a piece of cake. I kicked extra points in junior high." Steve beelined it to the meeting point, assuming that if he were the first one there, he would get to kick first.

They were supposed to start the contestants at the thirty-five-yard line, but the person directing the contest got confused and teed the ball up at the ten-yard line. "This will be the easiest $250 I have ever earned," thought Steve. He lined up, approached the ball, connected—and off it flew towards the bleachers.

After one year at Weber State, Amy was taking Saltines with her to every class, hoping she wouldn't throw up before class was over. Steve and Amy were going to be parents.

The little pink house was cute, but very little. In a few months, it would be too small. Steve and Amy started looking for a new home. With their daytime hours packed with work and school, they did a fair share of tromping through the snow and peering into new-builds with a flashlight at 10:00 p.m. Eventually, they found the perfect house about five miles west of Clearfield, in Syracuse.

A few months later, on a Sunday morning, Amy kept looking out the front window. Steve had gone to a church meeting. He should have been home by now. All the other neighbors were home. Finally, Amy called their friend who lived across the street. "Rick, do you know where Steve is?"

"Is it time?" shouted Rick.

"It's time."

Minutes later, Rick was speeding to the church building to retrieve Steve. Ten minutes later, Steve was home. An hour later, they were a family of three.

Steve and Amy were besotted with Steffany. When Steffany was about three weeks old, Scott Parker, Steve's close friend from his mission, visited the Hardisons for the weekend.

"Scott. Scott. Wake up. I want to show you something."

"What? . . . Huh?. . . Steve, what time is it?"

"Does it matter?" asked Steve. "Look how beautiful this baby is."

Scott looked over at the clock. It was 2:30 a.m. He groaned. Steve was euphoric.

Steffany conveniently arrived between the summer and fall quarters. Amy had twenty-seven more credit hours until she got her bachelor's degree. This was decades before online classes, so Amy arranged with her professors to take some of her classes as home study. Others she took at night. When she had to go to the campus to take a test, Steve took Steffany with him to his class. He became known as "the business guy with the baby."

A Diagnosis

Steve was consuming an inordinate amount of food, day and night. He was drinking gallons of liquid. His preferred beverage was milk, but that much milk stressed their budget, so he switched to Kool-Aid.

When they got married, Steve weighed 200 pounds. At 6'4", he was spare. Over the past few months, he had dropped over forty pounds. Now he was skeletal. He finally agreed to visit the student health center. They sent him straight to the hospital. A glucose tolerance test revealed a blood sugar of 832, eight times that of a non-diabetic. Steve was diagnosed with juvenile-onset (type 1) diabetes.

The transition was not an easy one. With a colossal metabolism, Steve had been able to do things most people can't, like eat half of a Texas Sheet cake in one sitting, without gaining weight. He loved that, but he could give it up. The bigger issue was that Steve hated to stop when he was in his flow, which was almost always. He hated to deal with little details, like eating. Steve loved extremes—black and white, on or off, all or nothing. He loved a pedal-to-the-metal life. Managing diabetes was all about balance and moderation. This was going to cramp his style.

National Extemporaneous Speaking Competition

Steve was sitting at the airport in Salt Lake City, waiting to board his flight to Washington, DC. He thought back on the events that had gotten him here.

It started in his business class when his professor announced a speaking competition sponsored by the business fraternity. Steve didn't think much about it. His mind was on other things, like making his $800 that month. A couple of days later, his professor pulled him aside. "Steve, you haven't signed up for the competition yet."

"I know. I wasn't planning on it."

"Steve, I really think you should. This would be a great opportunity. You will do well in the extemporaneous speaking category. I *really* think you should sign up."

So he did. He won first place and advanced to the state level.

As the representative from Weber State, Steve went up against the winners from Brigham Young University, Utah State, University of Utah, and Southern Utah State. Steve hadn't prepped for the match up and he definitely hadn't worried about it. Talking the birds out of the trees—what could be more fun?

When Steve took second place for the state of Utah and learned that the state winner went on to compete at the national level in Washington, DC, he started to realize that maybe this was a big deal. Two days before the competition, Steve got a phone call. The first-place winner for Utah was sick. Could Steve take her place? Absolutely.

The competition started out with a Friday evening meet-and-greet. As Steve scanned the room and the contestants, he observed a man approaching him. He was preppy, polished, and wore a $2,000 suit. The man put out his hand and asked, "What school are you from?"

"Weber State."

"Where's that?"

He turned away before Steve could say "Utah," or ask him what school he was from, but Steve heard him as he introduced himself to another participant: Harvard.

As Steve moved about the room, he heard the names of all the ivy league schools. He heard surnames of people he heard about on television. There was no missing the man who made sure everyone knew his father was a U.S. senator.

"This is a big deal," thought Steve. His blue eyes turned steely. "I am winning this thing."

The next day, Steve advanced through four rounds of competition. He and four others moved on to the finals. The finalists were isolated in different rooms. Fifteen minutes before they were to speak, they were given the question: "If there was one thing you could do to change the world, what would you do?"

"This is so over," laughed Steve. "I have been thinking about this question my whole life. I thought about it in the shed. I grappled with it on my mission. I know exactly what I am going to say." He approached the microphone:

> If there were one thing, and only one thing, I could do to change the world, I would change all the sacred texts that teach the world must end with an Armageddon or some cataclysmic battle. I would change all the holy scriptures that say one group of people has the truth and another doesn't. I would change what parents teach their children so that any teachings that divide and alienate people of different races, religions, and countries vanished overnight. In their place I would insert the teaching that all people are equal. All people are valuable. When we come together to work for the common good of all people, we have community instead of

separation. We have unity instead of divisiveness. We have love instead of hate.

Steve won first place. It was a big deal.

The phone rang. Amy picked up.

"Guess who is the National Extemporaneous Speaking Champion of 1980?" asked Steve.

"Are you serious? You're not joking?" squealed Amy. "Tell me all about it."

Steve gave Amy the blow by blow. He recreated his winning speech.

"I am so proud of you," Amy said. "This is amazing. You are amazing. Congratulations!" They reveled in his accomplishment—but not for too long. Long-distance phone calls were expensive. Amy hung up. She stared at the phone, thinking, *That isn't what we believe. Is this going to be a big deal?*

Chapter 9

From Proctor & Gamble to Xerox

Steve scanned the notices on the bulletin board in the business department. Zions Bank . . . Bonneville Communications . . . Proctor and Gamble. Proctor and Gamble? The maker of Pampers, Tide, and Crest. This American icon was coming to Weber State to interview? This just might be the career path he was looking for.

On the morning of his interview, Steve shined his shoes, adjusted his pocket scarf three times, and took a final glance in the mirror. He had a few butterflies, but they were the good kind—butterflies pumped with confidence.

"So, Mr. Hardison, you are all set to graduate in May?" asked Mr. Smith.

"No. I don't graduate for one more year," responded Steve.

Mr. Smith almost concealed his annoyance. "Mr. Hardison, we aren't interviewing juniors."

"Mr. Smith, are you familiar with Weber State's basketball team?"

"No. But what does that have to do with anything?"

"They start three juniors and two sophomores. Can you imagine if the administrators told the coach he had to start a senior, just because he was a senior, even though it would weaken the team? There is someone in your organization that would want to hire me, even as a junior."

There was one person who could do that. They flew him in. He hired Steve on the spot. They offered Steve his choice of three territories. One happened to be Mesa, Tempe, and Scottsdale, Arizona. Steve's mom still lived in Arizona, and all of Amy's family lived there. It was an easy decision. Steve reminded Amy that they were headed to P&G's ivory tower. Arizona was a temporary stop.

Steve, Amy, and fifteen-month-old Steffany relocated to Arizona. They bought a new-built house and lived with Amy's parents for a month while it was finished. Steve would finish up his degree at Arizona State University. They were elated.

Steve's start date was January 15. Amy was excited all day to see how his first day went. Steve walked in at 5:00. She took one look at his face and her stomach dropped.

Steve said, "I made a big mistake."

Amy thought, "We just signed on a house."

Steve continued, "This isn't sales. I am a glorified stock boy. I put diapers on shelves. Nothing I do makes a difference in how many diapers the grocery store orders. That is all handled by management. It is a waste of my talents."

Steve stuck with it for six months while he looked for another job. The best part of the job was he could keep the damaged boxes of diapers. This was helpful, because Amy and Steve had another one on the way.

Steve's next job was at Safe and Sound, a mom-and-pop business that sold and installed alarm systems. It wasn't ideal. It was a stop-gap job to get him out of P&G before it drove him crazy.

Safe and Sound shared office space with another business. One day, a Xerox rep came in and pitched a copier to someone in the other business. Sitting at his desk, Steve watched the whole thing.

"That's the worst sales presentation I've ever seen," he thought. He picked up the telephone and made a call.

A perky voice greeted him. "This is Jody. Welcome to Xerox."

"Jody, can you tell me who's responsible for sales in your company?"

Steve was transferred to Helen Hermann. Steve told Helen what he had just observed. She invited him to come down to the Xerox offices. After they spoke, Helen offered Steve a job.

The environment at Xerox was fun and competitive. Most importantly, Steve was really selling. Compared to having doors slammed in his face in England, cold-calling local businesses was a walk in the park.

It wasn't long before Steve was selling twenty, thirty, and sometimes even forty copiers every month. The average was five to ten. Often, Steve was number one on the leader board for sales. This was clearly the kind of sales he loved.

In 1981, Steve's friend, Rick Glauser, sent him the book *How to Solve All Your Money Problems Forever: Creating a Positive Flow of Money Into your Life* by Victor Boc. Amy read it first. When

Steve came home from work that day, she met him at the door. Her first words were, "You are going to love this book. It isn't just about money. It is about thinking."

Steve picked up the book and flipped through the pages. "I'll eat later," he called out as he settled into the recliner and imbibed the book. By morning, he had read it twice.

This was everything he loved. Ideas were popping. Steve took out an ad in the local paper. It read simply: "Do you need some help solving a problem? Do you need someone to talk to? If so, call me. Steve."

Steve got a few calls. Talking to people and helping them with their problems—what could be more fun?

Steve opened his journal and wrote:

November 18, 1981

I am looking forward to developing a company by the name of Thought Process Inc., a concept in mind teaching. I think this will be big one day. I plan on setting up an office in my home for one-on-one instruction."

A thought? A vision? A dream?
A future.

Chapter 10

Rodel

Steve was getting restless. He was tired of selling copiers. Mike Koether invited Steve to join his startup, but that didn't feel quite right.

"It's going to be great," said Mike. "Are you sure?"

Steve nodded.

"Then I want you to meet my friend, Don Budinger. We were fraternity brothers at Notre Dame. He and his brother have a company that polishes silicon wafers. His brother is over manufacturing and Don is over sales. He could really use someone with your talents, and you will love him."

Steve and Don met at an upscale restaurant in Scottsdale. Don was impeccably dressed. He was polished, articulate, and charming, a modern-day Cary Grant. "This is someone I need to know," thought Steve.

Not long into their conversation, Don leaned forward and said,

"Steve, what would it take for you to come work for me?"

Steve named a figure. Don upped it. "You will start in sales, but that isn't where you'll stay." Don pulled out his pen and sketched an organizational chart of his company, Rodel. In the box labeled "General Manager," he wrote "Steve."

After a few false starts, Steve was finally in the job of his dreams.

Steve had a lot to learn. He didn't have a background in engineering or a Ph.D. in chemistry, like many of the Rodelians. He couldn't even read the products brochure without a dictionary. On one occasion, Steve was in a manufacturing facility and started to put his finger into some liquid. A stunned engineer pulled Steve's hand away just before he submersed it in a vat of hydrochloric acid.

Indeed, Steve had a lot to learn, but he knew how to go about it. He went into the plant in Delaware and talked to the people who worked on the assembly lines. He asked questions about how the products were made and how they worked. He asked the line workers what they needed to make their job easier. He went into the Research and Development lab, gowned up, and learned how to use the polishing machine. Steve spent more time at the plant than any salesperson ever had.

Steve mastered the nuts and bolts. Then he brought in his expertise: how to bring warring parties to consensus, how to listen for answers, and how to enroll people in a vision. He brought creativity and pit bull tenacity to solving problems. If salespeople complained that they couldn't get a foreign customer because they only bought from local vendors, Steve's response was, "It doesn't matter. We have to be better than whatever is in the way."

In 1986, Steve was promoted to national sales manager. One day, Mike Kulus, one of Rodel's salespeople, came into his office. "This is not good," said Mike as he slumped into a chair. "MEMC just fired us."

"What's going on?" asked Steve.

"They say our products are scratching their wafers and ruining their yields."

"Are they?"

Mike winced and gave a defeated nod. "They are going to find a new supplier."

"The world's largest manufacturer of silicon wafers and one of our biggest customers is taking their business to a competitor?" said Steve. "Get two plane tickets to St. Peters, Missouri, this afternoon, if possible."

"I don't think you understand," Mike responded. "They aren't happy. They don't want to see us. Ever."

"Just get the tickets," Steve said.

They flew out the next morning.

When they got to the corporate headquarters, they were given fifteen minutes to plead their case. Steve looked at the executives gathered around the conference table. They had scowls on their faces. Their arms were crossed. Steve and Mike were in hostile territory.

Steve took a deep breath and began, "We came to apologize. You have every right to be angry. You have every right to fire us. However, as I see it, you have two options. You can keep us, and we can work together as partners, or you can fire us and get another vendor—but you will have the same problem with the new vendor. This is an industry-wide problem. You're so zealous in guarding your intellectual property, we don't know how you use our product.

If you let us put an engineer in-house, right in your manufacturing facility, we can work together to get you what you need."

Steve watched their hands go from clenched to propping up their chins, as if thoughts of possibility needed support. The CEO slapped his hand on the table. "I like it."

They put a Rodel engineer in their plant. They improved the flatness of their wafers. They salvaged the partnership. Steve was promoted to president of Rodel Products Corporation, the sales arm of Rodel Products.

Steve was flying back from Delaware. The five-hour flight gave him time to reflect over the past eight years. He'd had great experiences with MEMC, Intel, Motorola, and Texas Instruments. He'd had a role in creating the joint venture of Rodel-Nitta in Japan. He had been integral in the merger of Rodel and Rodel Products. One of the highlights was definitely his relationship with Don.

For a boy below the tracks, he had done well. Granted, it took some time to rewrite some of his early scripts. He smiled when he remembered trying to convince Don that buying dress shirts from Walmart was a good thing. Don had shifted Steve's thinking. He had taught him abundance mentality. He had introduced him to a more refined world.

The amazing thing is Don had polished him up without changing his essence. Steve was still Steve. He worked hard and laced his work with fun. He pressed the edges. He was creative. He was unconventional.

Life was good. His future with Rodel was bright. Steve closed his eyes and fell asleep.

He didn't know the good times wouldn't last.

Chapter 11

Werner

Steve and Amy were staying at a local resort, celebrating their tenth wedding anniversary. At 2:00 a.m., Steve woke up in incredible pain. He picked up the hotel phone and dialed his friend and dentist, Dr. Andy Shumway. Andy picked up on the first ring.

"Are you awake?" asked Steve.

Andy, coincidentally, was awake, and offered to meet Steve at his dental office.

While Andy performed an emergency root canal, he told Steve about a remarkable patient. Every time she came in, she talked about something called "The Forum," the brainchild of a man named Werner Erhard. Andy was animated. He was going to attend the next Forum. Would Steve like to go with him?

The Forum? Steve had never heard of it. Would he like to go? Absolutely.

The day after his root canal, Steve registered for the next Forum in Phoenix. It was in four weeks. The Forum staff—all volunteers—phoned Steve on multiple occasions to confirm the location and the directions, and to ask Steve what he wanted to get out of his Forum. "This is overkill," thought Steve. "Just give me the address. I'll show up." The third time they called, Steve told them to leave him alone. "I know how to get there. You've got my money. I'm coming." He hung up on them.

When Steve arrived, he walked up to the registration area, where several tables held three hundred name tags. Steve looked for his name tag, twice. He turned to one of the volunteers and said, "I can't find my name tag."

"I can help you. What is your name?"

"Steve Hardison."

Heads popped up. The volunteer found his name tag. It was set off, all by itself on a separate table.

A different volunteer, Nancy Groben, approached. "Hi, Steve. We're going to give you a refund for The Forum. We don't think you would get much out of it."

"What are you talking about?" demanded Steve.

"You haven't taken it seriously."

Was Steve being kicked out of the course? Before it even started?

"What would I need to do to stay?" Steve asked. As if on cue, a small, dark-haired woman wearing a name tag that said "Linda" stepped in. Linda was crisp and clear about what he needed to do and who he needed to be. Steve liked her precision. He agreed and found a seat in the front row. Moments later, the Forum leader made her way to the front of the room. It was Linda.

After a short introduction, Linda stepped down from the stage, and walked through the audience. She called on a woman sitting next to Steve and engaged in a conversation with her. The woman described her brutal home environment, the tense atmosphere, and her difficult partner. She began crying.

The participants squirmed. Some looked like they wanted to jump up and hug the woman.

"Is this the bullshit you pull on your husband?" Linda said without emotion.

The woman stopped crying immediately. "Yes," she said coolly. Steve was enthralled. Here was candor that cut to the core. By the first break, Steve was certain of one thing: this was the best thing he had ever attended in his life. This was transformation with teeth. This was commitment to possibility so big that it was borderline ruthless. This was in-your-face, wake-you-up transformation. This was holding people accountable with grit. This was being your word. This was like coming home.

Within a few months, Steve had shared The Forum with hundreds of people. Steve and Amy went on to participate in multiple seminars and events. Steve continued to study Werner's material for ten years. He continued to share The Forum and its next iteration, Landmark. Stepping into The Forum was a pivotal moment in Steve's life. And he had come so close to getting chucked out.

Chapter 12

The Build-Up

His voice had an edge. He snarled at Amy. Maurine's head snapped up. Steve stormed out of the room. "You know, Amy," said Maurine, "that's not acceptable. You need to let him know that." It was out of character for Maurine to say anything that edged into how Steve and Amy lived their life.

"He doesn't do it often. He must have something going on."

Indeed, he did have something going on. But it was not a passing frustration. Steve was starting to come unwound.

Amy thought back to when she and Steve dated. He had disclosed that he had a bad temper when he was a kid. He threw bats when umpires called a third strike. He punched holes in walls. But these were things of the past. He had mastered his anger on his mission.

Now, twelve years post-mission, Amy was starting to sense that perhaps "master" wasn't the right word. He had shrunk it, like radiation shrivels a tumor. It had gone into remission. But evidence of a relapse was surfacing.

It wasn't just anger. Steve had a lot gurgling inside of him. He was traveling a week or two each month, flying to Delaware, Silicon Valley, Cincinnati, and Japan for business. Travel messed with Steve's blood sugar and it required Steve to handle details. So many details. And paperwork. And life's minutiae. They buried Steve. He could do things no one else could do, and the things most people could do crushed him. Plus, Steve burned bright. To rekindle, he needed down time and space. Lots of it. His walls were closing in.

When he was at Rodel in Scottsdale, Steve started going to the park and taking naps during his lunch hour. These weren't power naps to recharge; these were escapes into oblivion for survival. On Sunday nights he started going to bed at 7:00 p.m. The house needed to be pin-drop quiet. Amy lay by him and rubbed his arm. He was on edge about the workweek starting. His nerves were amped on anxiety.

Four kids. A wife. A job. An avalanche of details. Soul-sucking travel. Questions about faith. Building a custom home. Feeling unappreciated. Monotony. Ruts.

Steve was a pressure cooker. He was going to blow. The question was when.

Chapter 13

Demolition

Steve was sitting in a Landmark Forum seminar. Lloyd Fickett was standing at the front of the room, leading the seminar. With a salt and pepper beard trimmed close to his face, Lloyd had a professorial look. He was articulate and astute. He was explaining the concepts of enrollment and impeccability, as defined by Werner Erhard. He had learned them while working for Werner in San Francisco.

"My job was to make sure all the telephone cords were consistently straight and untangled on every phone, on every desk in the seven-story building."

Steve remembered telephone cords. They tethered the user to the wall or desk. A long cord granted a little freedom to roam, but was prone to tangle. He remembered his mom standing on a chair and holding the phone cord high above her head with the handset of the phone dangling. The handset twisted one way then the other, as if it were doing pirouettes. When it stopped spinning, the kinks were mostly gone.

"I could not run around the building straightening every cord after every call," said Lloyd. "I had to enroll every person into the commitment of untangled cords. I had to get them to see that impeccability exists in the smallest of actions."

"Here's a person who could get alignment into a company culture," thought Steve. "He's perfect for Rodel."

The next day, Steve talked to Don about hiring Lloyd as an executive coach.

"I'm not sure we need an outsider to come in and help us," Don protested. "Plus, Lloyd is expensive,"

"Don, we need him *because* he is from the outside. He can see things we can't."

Lloyd was engaged to work with the Rodel executive team. He started with Steve.

Lloyd entered Steve's office at Rodel and closed the door. He held his tightly-clenched fists in front of his chest and said, "Steve, what's this about?"

"What are you talking about?" asked Steve.

Lloyd raised his eyebrows. It was so obvious. Lloyd came at it from another direction. "You're constantly on edge and stressed. What's behind that?"

"Nothing's behind it. It's just the way I am."

Lloyd continued, "Who we are is created by a series of experiences and our decisions about those experiences. Over time, these form our fundamental approach to life. I have a process that will take you back to these early experiences so you can heal them. I do it in two sessions, one week apart. Are you interested?"

Steve was all in.

Steve arrived for his first session the next Friday evening. Lloyd and a gentleman named Ron sat in Lloyd's home office. They both had yellow legal pads. Steve took a seat in the middle of the room.

"When were you born?"

"How many siblings do you have?"

"What do you remember about. . . ?"

Lloyd's voice was calm. His questions were constant, like an escalator. For three hours, Lloyd queried, Steve responded, and Ron and Lloyd captured Steve's answers on paper.

After his final question, Lloyd flipped to the first page of the legal pad and began to read Steve's answers back to him.

"Your uncle constantly told you that you would never amount to anything."

"You were jumped by a group of teenagers and beaten up, egged on by a family member."

"There was the young-adult man who preyed on younger boys."

There were some darker things, too.

Steve felt dazed. He knew about those things. He had lived those things. But when they were all laid out with their jagged edges exposed, with his soul naked, there was no pretending it didn't matter. There was no imagining it was a one-off. So many people had injured him. No one had protected him. No wonder he was angry.

When the first process was complete, Steve drove a few streets away and parked under a tree. He felt like he did years ago when a water-ski had bashed in his bottom teeth, laying them flat and leaving the nerves exposed to the cold air. Only now his whole body was his teeth.

July 17, 1991. Round two. Steve knocked on the office door. A very pregnant woman greeted him warmly. Lloyd introduced her as Carrie and explained she was there to hold the space of love and to guide Steve in some breathing exercises.

Steve was surprised to see a large mattress on the floor of Lloyd's office. He was more surprised when Lloyd said it was for him and invited him to lie down.

Lloyd picked up the list of last week's questions and responses. He read the list slowly, pausing to ask Steve how he felt and if there was anything he wanted to say. There was so much to say, but Steve felt like he was in a war zone, taking incoming fire. How do you talk when you're dodging shrapnel?

Lloyd read Steve's words describing the experience of having his ear bitten, gnawed, and twisted by a family member. It had happened over and over until Steve's ear became grotesquely misshaped, like a pixie ear. He had to have surgery to fix it. The memory was so real Steve's ear started throbbing.

Carrie touched Steve's ear.

Steve screamed. It was primal and raw. He bolted to his feet.

"Stay on the mattress!" Lloyd called.

Steve dropped down. He thrashed. He kicked. His foot connected with Lloyd's file cabinets. The wood splintered.

Lloyd looked around, searching for a fire break. He tossed Steve a couple of legal pads. He ripped them up. Lloyd gave Steve a phone book, but it was too big to destroy. Steve tossed it.

This isn't working, thought Lloyd. *I have to take a different approach.* He took a deep breath and got down on the floor and wrapped his arms around Steve. It was like embracing fire. He whispered, "Steve, there's nothing left for you to prove. You're okay. Everything's all right. There's nothing left to prove."

Steve gulped for air, for life. They rocked back and forth. Back and forth. Finally, Steve's breathing slowed. He sagged into Lloyd's arms.

"Steve, this is rebirth," whispered Lloyd, "with all the pain and joy. Let the joy in."

For two hours, Lloyd guided Steve into a new state of being, a place where resentment and pain were not always suited up, ready for action. He restored Steve. He reoriented him. They went for a walk in the desert. Everything looked different. They ate lunch together. Everything tasted different.

As soon as Steve got in his car to drive home, he picked up his phone to dial Amy. He couldn't wait to share his breakthrough. But the more he shared, the more his peace evaporated. By the time he got home, all he could remember was his pain. Steve folded into the fetal position. He stared at the wall for the rest of the day, and the night, and the weekend.

On Monday morning, Steve clawed his way out of bed and showed up at Rodel. Each day devoured another piece of his soul. After six months, Steve went to Don and told him he had to quit. Don offered him thirty days off. Steve took them. For thirty days, he sat and stared and cried. It bought him ninety more days at Rodel, but it tarnished his golden boy image.

It hardly mattered. Steve had nothing more to give Rodel. He barely had enough to live.

Lloyd helped negotiate Steve's departure. It was complicated. Steve was an integral part of Rodel. The employees looked to him for inspiration and leadership. There was deep affection, even love, on both sides. They had been in the trenches together. And money was involved. How could it not be complicated?

The details were handled, the dissolution achieved.

What were Steve and Amy going to do with the house they had just moved into, the one they had been building for two years? What were they going to do with their lives?

The future looked bleak.

Chapter 14

The Birth of Coaching

Steve was sitting on the deck, staring out at the mountains. He had been doing that a lot over the past few months. If only he could unplug forever. He wondered what would win, his pain or his responsibility for his wife and four children. It was rock-paper-scissors.

Steve had a modest severance package from Rodel, but with no income, his savings were like an air mattress with a slow leak. How long before it was flat? They could sell the house, but that would be a temporary solution. At some point, Steve would have to do something to provide.

When Steve was at Weber State, he was constantly being recruited for multi-level marketing. He ticked all the boxes. He was dynamic, bold, and gregarious. He loved sales. Steve knew he would have done well. He was sure of it. But Amy wasn't on board. He still resented that she had clipped his wings. Maybe he should give it a try. Amy was worried enough about him to offer no resistance.

Steve stepped into multi-level marketing. It was a disaster. He learned that he was not constituted to nudge, encourage, and prod people who weren't serious, or who needed support every step of the way. Hand-holding drove him crazy.

He stepped right back out. The foray into multi-level marketing had consumed some of their precious savings, but Steve now knew without a doubt that it was not for him.

Steve was at the car wash. As usual, he was talking with people. He met Keith, who was struggling with his business. By the end of the conversation, Keith was Steve's first coaching client. He came to Steve's house. They sat at the dining table and Steve helped him solve his problems. Steve saw a glimmer of possibility. It was enough to break the white-knuckled grip of despair. It was enough to tap into hope.

Steve's phone rang. It was Bill Brebaugh, Steve's former boss at Xerox. He was currently the sales manager at the University of Phoenix.

"Hi, Steve. Have you heard of a company named TimeMax?"

"No."

"They are a corporate training company that specializes in time management. They're only about ten minutes away from you. They've done some work with us and I really, really like them. I think they could use you."

A few days later, Dennis Deaton, the co-owner and CEO of TimeMax, was sitting at Steve's dining table. Steve asked Dennis questions about the structure of his company and what he wanted to accomplish. Dennis said something about his partner.

"A partner? Why isn't he here?" asked Steve.

Dennis's answer revealed far more than he had intended.

In ten minutes, Steve, Dennis, and Reece Bawden were sitting together at TimeMax. Steve quickly got to the heart of the matter. "If you want to fix your problems at TimeMax, you will have to trust each other and talk to each other. The first step is to deal with why that isn't happening." Steve then gave them an irresistible offer. Steve would work with them for six weeks without being paid. At the end of six weeks, they could decide whether or not to hire him.

Steve knew that six weeks was long enough to create miracles.

Steve and Reece were sitting at the conference table. "Reece, how much business do you do with Motorola?"

"They're our biggest customer."

"What is their process for enrolling employees into our courses?"

"Actually," said Reece, "I don't know."

"I think we should find out," said Steve.

Reece shifted in his chair and tapped the table with his fingers. "I am the president of TimeMax. Am I supposed to walk into Motorola's human resources department and just start asking questions about their protocol?"

"No. All you have to do is watch."

A few days later, Steve shook the hand of Motorola's training development manager. "Hi. I'm Steve Hardison and this is Reece Bawden from TimeMax. I'm his coach. Could you help us understand something? We have one-hundred and twenty seats available in the courses we put on for Motorola, but only thirty people come. When we talk to your employees after a course, they say they loved the course and they had to wait for two months to get in because it was sold out. But we are definitely not at capacity. Could you walk us through how someone from Motorola gets into our courses?"

"Sure. The Motorola employee comes to us and tells us what training they want. We look in the computer and see how many seats are available." She clicked a few keys on her keyboard. "We have thirty seats available for TimeMax. When those are filled, we don't put anyone else in."

Steve asked, "Who puts the 'thirty' in the computer?"

"I do."

"Can we change that to 125?" asked Steve.

Click.

Done.

As they drove back to TimeMax, Reece said, "Steve, Motorola buys fifty courses each year." Reece did a quick calculation in the air. "Do you realize that putting one hundred more employees in each course, could net an increase of $1,125,000?"

"Yep," said Steve. "And that's just one conversation." He almost added, "Not a bad miracle for starters."

Steve asked Reece to come to their next meeting with the top three things he wanted to handle.

"I can tell you that right now. We want to handle our debt."

"Who do you owe money to?"

"Well, there's the binder manufacturer, but we have forty-five days before that bill is due."

"Don't those venders want payment in thirty days?" asked Steve.

"Yes, but I negotiated one hundred and eighty days."

"One-hundred and eighty days! You're taking advantage of him. Put him at the top of the list. Who else?"

They listed every outstanding account. Before they finished, Steve again asked if there was anyone else that needed to be on their list.

"Well," said Reece, "there is one more debt. We owe $80,000 to an elderly woman."

"When is the money due?" asked Steve.

"There is no date."

"Get her on the phone."

After a few pleasantries, Steve asked her when she planned on being paid.

"Oh, whenever they can," she said. "I just love those boys."

"How about in thirty days, on July 1?" responded Steve.

"Oh, that's fine. But there's no hurry. It doesn't matter."

"It matters to us," said Steve. "We are trying to clean up our ship." They gave their word for July 1.

"Steve," asked Reece. "How are we going to pay all these vendors?"

"We're going to sell our way out of debt."

"But we don't really have a sales force. Brent is the only one who sells. A few other people help a little, when they have time."

"My point exactly. We need a sales force. Let's get started."

Steve, Reece, and Dennis were reviewing what they had accomplished together over the past five years.

"We made a lot of changes, especially that first year, which ruffled a few feathers," said Dennis.

Reece smiled. He would have chosen a stronger expression. At times, it was almost a mutiny. Some people preferred their old way of doing business: softer, friendlier. . . ineffective.

"Our business profits soared," said Reece. "Our personal incomes doubled each year for the first three years." Reece paused for a moment. "But your biggest impact wasn't financial. Do you know I keep a list of leadership principles I have learned from you? I use those principles at TimeMax, at church, and with my family.

"So many times, you listened to me for five minutes and then spent the next hour helping me see the thinking that caused the problem in the first place. That has changed me forever. It has changed how I think. It has changed who I am. I will be forever grateful."

Steve had changed a lot too. Five years ago, he had been sitting on his deck, starring at the mountains, mired in depression. He had reached the end of his winning formula. Issues from his childhood clamored for resolution. The exercise with Lloyd had jarred his soul. All these things collided at one time. It was almost too much.

Almost, but not quite.

As Lloyd promised, Steve had experienced a rebirth. He started resolving his past. He created a new way to win. He embraced without apology the man he was at his core: outrageous, bold, committed, loving, unleashed, unorthodox, and brashly confident.

With newfound clarity, Steve 2.0 was ready to roll.

Chapter 18

Steve Chandler

The employee sat at the conference table staring at the white board. There wasn't anything on it. His shoulders sagged. His eyes were dull.

"You can do this," he said to himself. "This isn't as hard as bankruptcy . . . or kicking addiction." He wasn't buying it. This seemed worse. There isn't a twelve-step program for you when you have a wife with mental illness.

Steve Chandler thought of signing the papers that would institutionalize his wife. He had to do it. It was the most merciful thing he could do. She couldn't function outside, in the real world. He couldn't afford private care. As it was, he had borrowed money from TimeMax to help with her expenses. "For all the good it did me. Now I have four kids to raise, a wife who is institutionalized, *and* I'm in debt to the company I work for." He groaned.

It would be so easy to be swallowed up.

Someone was talking. He looked up. It was that new guy, the one Reece and Dennis had hired as a coach. "Were you talking to me?"

"Yes," said Steve.

"Oh."

Steve waited for a minute, but Chandler had sunk back into his pain. "I asked what you are doing."

"What difference does it make? You don't care about people like me," Chandler responded.

"How do you know who I care about?" Steve challenged.

"Fair point. Okay. You're a problem solver. See what you can do with this. I work as a salesperson—and I hate sales."

"If you could do anything," asked Steve, "what would you do?"

"I would write books and I would speak."

"Have you done either of those things?"

Chandler shook his head.

"You do realize that you work for a company that sells speaking and training?" said Steve.

"I asked the company president if I could be a speaker, and he said no."

"One guy tells you that you can't speak, and you quit? You'll have to do better than that," said Steve. "Look, I'll arrange for the room, and you can speak next Thursday night."

Chandler swallowed. Could he overcome crippling stage fright in one week? What if he stepped into his dream job and failed? Would he ever get another chance like this? "I'll be there," said Chandler, but not very loudly.

On Thursday night, Steve Chandler showed up to speak. Steve Hardison showed up to listen. He was the entire audience. The next Thursday night, ten people came to listen to Chandler. One of the ten was Patrick Provost, Hardison's friend.

After Chandler's presentation, Patrick walked up to Hardison, "Hi, Bud."

"Thanks for coming, Patrick. What did you think?"

"Really?"

"Of course 'really.'"

"It was grim and dull."

"Yep. That is what I thought too. But mark my words. Steve Chandler will be a great speaker one day."

"Nowhere to go but up," replied Patrick.

Chandler walked into TimeMax with a bounce in his step. He had attended one of Landmark's personal development seminars the night before. It was about creating your future. When he saw Steve, he announced, "I now have a five-year plan for becoming a public speaker."

"If that's what you want, that's fine," said Steve.

"Is there something wrong?" asked Chandler.

"You could take five years to become a public speaker if you want. Or you could do it in five months."

"I'm not you, you know," Chandler said. "I have to take a public speaking course. I have to get over my stage fright. That takes time."

"That's all in your head."

It all seemed so logical, so real to Chandler. *Does Hardison always bend reality?* thought Chandler. *Would it be as pliable for me?* He was willing to find out.

Chandler passed out flyers to the businesses near TimeMax, inviting people to attend a free talk on achieving goals. He made up a booklet with some of his favorite quotes from Stephen Covey, Napoleon Hill, and Tony Robbins. Chandler would build a discussion on the quotes. Who could argue with the experts?

As a single father with no money for babysitting, his kids would have to attend. They would be their dad's official pencil runners and his unofficial cheerleaders.

To counter his stage fright, Chandler practiced his presentations whenever he could, at home, in the car, during dinner. Before his kids went to bed, he would gather them and say, "I want to give you one of my talks."

They groaned.

"Only for ten minutes. That's all," insisted Chandler.

Just as Chandler was hitting his stride, he was interrupted with "Dad, this is so boring."

"Count your blessings," he replied. "You only get ten minutes. Grownups get an hour."

One day, Steve read a booklet on fundraising that Chandler had cowritten before he worked at TimeMax. "This is amazing," he said to Chandler. "Why don't you present these ideas to the whole TimeMax team?"

Chandler blanched. "I could never stand in front of the whole company and speak."

"Of course you can," insisted Steve.

Chandler did it, but his nerves were espresso jittery.

When he finished, Steve was the first person to reach Chandler. "Out of the park!" Steve said, with a grin.

"I'm just glad it's over."

As Chandler gathered up his things, Steve stopped him. "Before you go, will you autograph my booklet?"

Chandler's eyes narrowed. "Are you mocking me?"

"I would never do that. I'm serious. I really want your autograph."

"Why?" asked Chandler. "After all, I'm in the company—and this isn't a real book."

"I want you to remember this moment," replied Steve. "Something miraculous is going to occur out of what you did today. You will be a world-famous speaker one day."

Chandler didn't believe him, but he signed anyway.

Dennis Deaton, CEO and co-founder of TimeMax, was TimeMax's primary speaker. His speaking schedule was full, yet requests were flooding in. Hardison recommended that Steve Chandler take the overflow.

Whenever Chandler spoke, Hardison attended. Afterwards, he would give Chandler feedback. "Don't try to be Dennis. Your resume and your experience don't support it. Be you. Let them hear about your failures. They will connect with you."

Chandler brought authenticity, humor, and scrappy wisdom to his presentations. People related. Within a year, his courses at TimeMax were selling out.

Soon, Chandler was flying around the country to give his presentations. Chandler represented TimeMax, but the content of his courses was his own. When Chandler went into corporations, he set his own prices and paid his own expenses.

One day, Steve and Chandler were sitting in the TimeMax conference room, looking at a map and discussing Chandler's out-of-state speaking schedule.

"Steve," asked Hardison. "How much are you charging when you speak?"

"$1,250 per event."

"Steve, you have to raise your prices," said Hardison.

Chandler shifted in his seat. "I don't want to raise my prices."

"But you can't even cover your travel expenses at $1,250. You're going in the hole," insisted Hardison. "You'll $1,250 yourself to death."

Chandler took a deep breath. "Well, what's my value?"

"I can't tell you your value. You have to determine that yourself. Then you deliver on the value you set. If I were you, I would charge $40,000."

Chandler choked. "But what if they won't pay $40,000? I would rather get $1,250 than nothing."

"Steve," said Hardison. "They will pay you $40,000. You're worth it."

Chandler wasn't so sure.

Shortly after this, Motorola approached Reece and Dennis and said they had a problem with morale on their line. Did TimeMax have some programs that addressed morale and culture? Dennis said, "No." Reece said, "No." Chandler said, "Yes." Dennis and Reece stared at him.

Chandler explained, "I . . . I have been working on developing a course to help people take ownership of their own morale and not make others, including their company, responsible for their attitude."

"When can we see it?"

They set up a time. Going for broke, they also invited several decision makers from Texas Instruments to come and observe. No one had any idea what Chandler was going to say. Motorola and Texas Instruments were big companies. They were important clients. It was risky to use them as guinea pigs. Reece and Dennis were nervous. Chandler hit it out of the park. The Texas Instrument execs wanted Chandler, and they wanted him in Texas. They adjourned to the conference room to work out the details. Chandler stood at the white board. He wrote $1,250 on the board and started to explain his fees.

Hardison interrupted. "Do you mind if I make it a little easier for you to see what Steve Chandler is saying? Steve charges $1,250 per person for his course. But if you put one hundred people in the room, we can get the price down so it's closer to $400 per person." They didn't bat an eye. They booked ten dates for $400,000. Chandler had a new fee for speaking: $40,000 a day.

Twenty-five years later, the conference room at the Sheridan was filled to capacity. Steve Chandler was there to speak. Steve Hardison was there to listen. Hardison arrived just as the man at the microphone was finishing his introduction.

". . . Steve Chandler is the author of over forty books, which have been translated into twenty-five languages. He has created in-person and online coaching schools that are in high demand. He is a highly sought-after speaker. We are lucky to have him here today." The audience rocketed to their feet and applauded for several minutes.

Chandler stepped to the mic. "Before I begin, I want to thank my coach, Steve Hardison, who is here today. Without him, I would not be here today. Hardison is known in coaching circles, and in business circles, and in personal growth circles and in any circle you can think of as 'The Ultimate Coach.' He coaches way beyond the normal concept of coaching. To call him a life coach is like calling The Beatles a garage band."

Steve Hardison and
Steve Chandler,
outside Hardison's
office, 2019

Part Two

The Ultimate Coach

Chapter 16

The Office

At first, Steve coached at his dining room table. It worked. By 8:00 a.m., the kids had left for school and Amy was ensconced in her office. It was private enough, but not ideal.

One day, late in 1993, Steve was puttering around his property and stepped into the storage room on the west end of his house. The kids' bicycles stood clustered, propped on their kickstands, like dominoes tempting fate. The lawnmower was parked to their side, flecked with grass. Tools were scattered on the work bench. It smelled like gasoline and paint. Steve saw possibility.

In a few months, with the help of Gary Gietz, a client and general contractor, glass-panel doors replaced the heavy utility doors. Lush cherrywood cabinetry displaced plywood storage shelves. A couch and leather chair sat where the bicycles and lawnmower had been.

The transformation was extensive. How apropos.

No Exceptions

When Steve was young, he envisioned wearing suits and flying around the world doing business. It's common enough today, if you substitute business casual (or Lululemon) for suits. It wasn't so common in 1965. In 2023, Steve still loves wearing suits, but not to work. He often walks into a coaching session wearing shorts and flip flops, or maybe loafers. One of the perks of living in Arizona is that such attire is weather-appropriate year-round. When he wants to gussy up for a session, he dons long pants and one of his sixty pairs of shoes, perhaps his favorite: patent leather magenta oxfords. He does not fly around the world to coach. His clients fly or drive to him. No exceptions.

Why is Steve so adamant about his clients traveling to him? Steve wants clients to have skin in the game. The greater the commitment, the greater the results. Steve charges a lot for his coaching. For some clients, that creates a sell-your-firstborn kind of commitment. For some clients, any fee at any price would be immaterial, but arranging their schedule to regularly be in Steve's office requires colossal commitment.

Many coaches offer coaching via Skype, FaceTime, Zoom, or some other video conferencing. It would be so much easier, so much more convenient. No long lines at airport security. No hours in the sky. But it wouldn't be the same. Steve knows this. So do his clients. One potential client from Argentina asked Steve if he would be willing to coach her through Skype.

His response was immediate: "No." She promptly wired money. She knew she had found the coach she was looking for.

Preparation

Steve's office is not simply a meeting place where coach A meets client B—a more private Starbucks. It is a sacred place. Succinctly stated, the word "sacred" means to take something from common use and dedicate it to a holy purpose. At all levels and in all domains, sacredness does not just happen. It is intentional.

The office has pearl-grey shag carpet. (Hardison has a soft spot for anything that reminds him of the 1970s.) Before any client enters, Steve himself rakes the carpet, starting at the far corner and walking backwards to the door. Each client steps into a fresh space. Stephen McGhee says, "Anytime I walked into that office, mine were the first footprints on that freshly raked carpet. I don't even think I realized it at first. I just knew that there was something different going on, like, 'I'm breaking ground here.'"

Without fail, when a client arrives, his or her flag is flying. Many clients start scanning for their flag while they are still on the freeway, approaching the exit that will take them to Steve's house. When they see their flag, they get a little jolt of bliss. They are royals in residence, at least for the next two hours.

There are two flagpoles at Steve's house, one by the front door and one in the backyard, near his office. Each client has a flag. It may be the flag of his university, state, or country. It may have a logo of his business or something he loves or something that characterizes the client. It may represent the client's vision or the essence of the work he or she is doing with Steve.

Lisa Berkovitz relates, "I arrived at his house and he had two flags flying for me, a Canadian flag and a 528 flag. I had shared with him that 528Hz is the frequency of love. It's the heart of my life's work. I am working on a global "528 project" that is about love-based businesses worldwide. It is my biggest vision."

What was the impact of seeing the flag of her country and the flag of her passion? Lisa says, "I feel he has my back in a way that I've never experienced, and he's holding me to my highest in a way that no one ever has."

Steve's preparation is not solely external: flying flags, raking carpet, getting the office at the right temperature, and setting out snacks and fruit. He prepares internally. He clears his mind. He clears his heart. He steps into his office ready to work miracles.

The preparation is mutual. Steve's clients have invested significant funds for the opportunity of sitting in his office with him. They have arranged their lives and their schedules to be there, sometimes flying across the country, sometimes flying from other countries. Some fly into Phoenix a day or two before their session to prepare, and some stay a few hours or a few days afterwards to digest their experience. Even if they are just driving across the valley, too much is at stake to just show up.

Jason Jaggard relates, "Getting ready to work with Steve Hardison is like preparing myself for travelling to Mecca. I have a special pen. I have a special notebook. There are all these things that I do to treat the process with the sacredness that it deserves."

That is the preparation once you have laid down money. You don't even get in the door without a considerable, upfront investment of time and effort. Jason shares his experience:

I reached out to a couple people whom I really admired for coaching. We talked for a little bit, and they said, "We would love to work with you, but we think that you would really,

really enjoy working with this guy Steve Hardison."

When I started talking to people about Hardison, I realized you say his name and it's like a hush falls over the crowd. So, I went to his website and checked him out.

I sent him a nice little email and said I would like to work with him. He said, "Great." Then he gave me a bunch of stuff to do. He sent me two books, not written by him, and said, "I want you to read these first. And I want you to read

Philip Weech, 2021

everything on my website. And I want you to watch these three hours of videos. And I want you to think about what it would be like for us to work together. Then get back to me."

It took me a month to do all these things. And then I reached back out to him, and we set up a time. Initially I thought he was creating hoops for me to jump through to see if I really wanted it. What I didn't realize until later was that he started serving me from the second that I reached out to him. I hired him two months after he and I initially talked. At my first actual session, I felt like I had already been working with him for two months for free.

Gina Carlson says, "Working with Steve is to go big or go home." Iyanla Vanzant put it this way: "Steve Hardison is not for the faint of heart, or the hopers, the wishers, the tryers. He's not for the dreamers. He's not for the wannabes. When you step into that experience, you've got to be ready. You've got to be ready to take your A game and throw it the hell out the window. Because in the presence of Steve Hardison, your A game ain't going to get you to first base."

Gifts

The most striking things in Steve's office are the gifts his clients have given him. These are not off-the-shelf gifts. They are unique and beautiful, but they were not chosen for their beauty. Some are prized possessions a client has given to Steve, like a Tibetan bowl the Dalai Lama had given to Dr. Alison Arnold. After working with Steve, she knew it belonged in his office.

All the gifts mean something. Some reflect the identity or the culture of the client. Some represent the work they do. Some become the work itself.

On a small table next to the client couch sits a red crystal heart from Tiffany's, given to Steve from Iyanla Vanzant. Steve cherishes it. It not only reminds Steve of Iyanla, it became his designated object to teach people that they are as powerful and capable as he is. It is a principle he has taught to many.

Steve Chandler vividly remembers sitting in his office when Steve said, "Anything I do, you could do. If I take this glass heart and throw it at the window, the window will break. If you pick up this glass heart and throw it at the window, the window will break.

Chandler recounts: "He was holding the heart. I thought, 'He's going to throw it at that window right now.' So I said, 'I really see that. Please put it down.' I knew he wouldn't hesitate to throw it at the window if he thought I wasn't getting the point."

Chandler didn't want to be responsible for the carnage.

Most who cross the threshold of the office feel something. Brandon Green wrote, "I found the office had a special energy to it. And I could tell, even without any additional information from Steve, that special work had happened in that room. It definitely had that feel."

Kai Jordan says:

I walked into his office and I was brought to tears. I could literally sense the miracles created in that room. I have had the privilege of being with Sadhguru, an enlightened master, for four years. I'm very familiar with yoga practices and spiritual masters and the quality of energy. But this was a different kind of energy. I could literally feel it. It was like I was hearing the whispers of the conversations that had happened in that room with Steve. It was moving.

When clients step into Steve's office, they enter a space of creation and transformation. It is a place for rebirth, healing lifelong wounds, and unleashing possibility. The work is so far-reaching that the conversations linger. They are palpable. Little wonder Steve's office shares borders with the sacred.

The Office

Chapter 17

Fasten Your Seat Belt

How do you describe Steve's coaching? Scott Parker says, "On his webpage, Steve says his coaching is not for the 'faint of heart.' That is a gross understatement. Bring a seat belt."

Dave Orton first heard of Steve in 2011. Two years later, he was driving up to his house to meet him for the first time. Recognizing that Steve was "a pretty important person," he had taken extra care in dressing. He hadn't brought a seat belt. He relates his experience:

> I came to this meeting wearing a suit and tie. I had polished my shoes and made sure that I looked really good. I walked into Steve's house and he offered me a piece of fruit. I had eaten recently, so I declined. We talked for a few minutes and then he looked at me with his piercing look and said,

"Dave, you're the most pretentious son of a bitch I've ever seen in my entire life."

What am I supposed to do with that?

The crazy thing about it was it was a statement of being, not a judgment. He wasn't saying, "Hey Dave, you're really bad because you're fake." He was acknowledging the importance that I had placed on my appearance and in showing up the way that I thought he thought I should show up, which was two times divorced from my reality.

Then we went to his office and talked for about three hours. We cut through the layers of bullshit that I had used to protect myself from the reality of life. I realized that I am as fake as can be with my wife. We created who I am now. That three-hour talk changed my life.

Karan Rai has also had seat-belt-wearing experiences with Steve. He says:

I had gone to Yale business school. I started on Wall Street. I was a CEO of a big company and a president of a second company. I was flying around in my own little plane. I had a house on the beach. I had a beautiful wife. I had a healthy child. I didn't go to Steve because I didn't know how to be successful. I went to Steve because I had done the things that I thought would make me successful—and I was miserable. My reason for going to him was to help me redefine success. I knew how to play this game called success. I had played it. I had won it. And I had lost. Obviously, I was playing the wrong game.

I told Steve that I had a really lucrative job and the only thing I was struggling with was trying to find a bit of happiness. I figured he would tweak a few things on the margins of my life and things would be good. Steve helped me see that part of the reason I wasn't happy is because I had traded who I really am for money. I wasn't doing it consciously, but I was doing it all the time.

I distinctly recall sitting with him one day and saying, "Steve, I think I'm in too deep. I think I'm making too much money. I'm too vested. I've been doing this for too long. I see my path. Another ten or fifteen years of doing this and I'm all set. I think I'm stuck."

Without blinking, he said, "Just burn it all down and build it again, this time the way you want to."

I said, "What are you talking about, old man?"

He was deadly serious.

"Doing more of what you're already doing is a waste of your time and a waste of my time. So, we have to figure out what we can do within you so you get to a place of joy and happiness in this situation. If you can't do that, then you have no choice but to burn it down and start over."

My homework assignment for the next month was to sit in solitude and silence and do the work to figure out if I was going to make the internal adjustments or build something from scratch on an ethos that I believe in. After a month of deep introspection, I knew what I had to do. I burned it down. That was the genesis of [our company] Asgard.

We're three years in and Asgard is doing great. We have two portfolio companies that we own directly, a third one that we own in partnership, and a fourth one that we're just getting ready to buy right now. All the businesses are doing well.

One of the things that contributes to the sense of a wild ride, the cinch-the-seat-belt experience of Steve's coaching, is that he does not have four or five different coaching plans, one for business, one for personal development, one for relationships, one for dreams. Scott Parker says, "Steve doesn't have a boilerplate template from which he works. He creates each session for each individual on the spot, as it happens. That is his genius."

James Malinousky lives in Vancouver, Canada. He attended Werner Erhardt's leadership course in Cancun. While there, he became good friends with another participant, Martine Cannon. She kept talking about her coach, Steve Hardison, and encouraging James to visit him. Eventually, James saw "this YouTube thing about an NFL player that Steve worked with." James was curious, so he picked up the phone and called Steve. He relates:

That first, live conversation was when he really grabbed me. I don't know what it was. He just had this pure, straight talk. It was like it was coming in me, or right through me. It was coming from his heart to mine. So, I hopped on a plane and flew to Phoenix for the day.

I went to his house and we got started. He didn't mess around. He got right into it, right there. There was no beating around the bush. I thought, "This guy is wild."

The way he was talking was really intense too. When you're sitting on the couch across from him, there's no hiding. He's reading right through you. There's no bullshit. It's like he's peeling you apart within ten minutes.

Iyanla Vanzant, a celebrated spiritual teacher, speaker, and host of *Iyanla: Fix My Life* on the Oprah Winfrey Network, shared her seat-belt moment with Dr. Alan D. Thompson, who conducted the interviews for *The Ultimate Coach* (original edition). Because Alan is Australian, Iyanla included some background information. She says:

Let me say something so that we can be very clear. I am a black woman out of the belly of Brooklyn. I don't know if you know about Brooklyn. If you're black, Brooklyn is the place you want to come from. Either Brooklyn or Chicago. They got black people all over, but Brooklyn, Harlem, Chicago—these are the places to come from.

Steve Hardison is a very tall white man. I think you may have noticed that. My encounters with him caused the slave chains of my ancestors to rattle in me because he represents everything that I was taught to be afraid of. He's male. He's white. He's big. He looks you in your eyes when he's speaking to you. You have to understand, my grandmother was a Native American raised in the South. Even though I had a college degree and a law degree, I was not to look at a white man. And I was terrified that Steve Hardison wouldn't let me speak to him unless I looked him in his eyes. So, when I met Steve Hardison, I was very clear we were going to heal something.

Steve is masterful at affirming people. He is also authentic. Steve Hardison would say to me, "You are powerful," "You are masterful," "You are gifted." Every time this big, white man would say something to me like "You are powerful," it would take me about three weeks to process that because my ancestral slave chains and my Native American bloodline could not receive that from a white man. As smart as I was, as accomplished as I was, he was accessing a cellular memory. He helped me move from that. It changed who I am as a person.

Changing your life often means grappling with ghosts from your past, probing the troubled relationships that shaped and wounded you, confronting the you you barely admit is there. It may mean burning it all down and starting again. Hardison is gifted at walking you through the journey.

But bring a seat belt.

Chapter 18

The Coaching Experience

"The first time I went to Steve Hardison's house I was with Steve Chandler's ACS (Advanced Client Systems) group. As much as I wanted to be present, I was in my mind about meeting this $200,000 coach. I'm going to walk into his house and I'm going to levitate, right?" So mused Devon Bandison.

What is it like to coach with Steve Hardison? There's talk on the street: He yells. He is intense. He throws people into his swimming pool. He will see into your soul. You will be transformed. He is like no other human being on the planet.

Of course, people exaggerate. He has never thrown a client into his swimming pool, and you won't levitate.

In considering the coaching experience, it is well to keep

Iyanla's words in mind: "Nothing that anyone has said, can say, or would say can describe the experience of coaching with Steve Hardison. Every experience is unique and authentic to who you are and what your spirit needs—not your mind, your heart, not even your soul, but your spirit." Consequently, Steve's coaching is the proverbial elephant with the blind men. Your experience depends on what part of the elephant you touch. Some clients get the tail, some get the ear, and some get the tusk.

Coachable clients usually touch the soft ear of the elephant. Jered Schager says, "I don't think he has an angry bone in his body." Norma Bachoura says, "I don't see Steve as that intense. I see him as a very soft guy. He is very sharp, but he is primarily gentle, as far as I'm concerned. My experience with him is that he's the gentlest person I have ever been with."

Sometimes Steve and his clients hit a sticky spot. The harder Steve has to work to get a client to hear him, the more he ratchets up. The resistance changes his delivery. Jason Jaggard says, "Steve's the only guy I know who can yell at you and be in love with you at the same time." Sometimes there is so much love that Amy can hear the ruckus at the other end of the house. It's the tusk.

Shanti Zimmerman has heard from many people that Hardison yells. She is okay with that. She observes, "He might have yelled in my presence, but I never felt like he was yelling at me. He's just really committed. There's no filter. He lays it out there. That *is* care, whether you get the blazing side or the softer side."

In spite of the fact that each person's experience is unique, there are some constants in coaching with Hardison. It is those constants that comprise this chapter. Some things, however, are too fundamental and too ample to share chapter space. They get their own chapters, which follow.

The Experience

Sitting with Steve in his office is not just a coaching session. It is an experience. Teresa Walding says, "When I met Steve, I was taken by his intensity and his directness. He leaned in and said, 'I want you to remember these words.' As it's turned out, I don't remember the words he said, but I remember the energy with which he said them. The experience was seared into my person—or my spirit, if you want to call it that." When it stopped sizzling, Teresa was left with "this extra-loving presence."

A Visceral Experience

Dr. Aaron Benes says, "My first session sitting with Steve was what Luke Skywalker must have felt like when sitting with Yoda for the first time. There was something about him that touched a very deep place within me. It was so powerful that it rattled my soul while pulling me forward at the same time."

Tom McGovern became aware of Steve through Dusan Djukich. Tom traveled from California to meet Steve. Tom says:

> We sat down and he started talking. Within two to five minutes, I'm crying my eyes out. I don't know why. Well, I do know why. It touched me in a way that I hadn't been touched in a really long time. As soon as I left, I called Dusan.
>
> He said, "What do you think?"
> I said, "I got to do it."
> "Do what?"
> "I got to coach with that guy. I just got to do it."

Before I met with Steve, I had no intention of flying from California to Arizona on a weekly basis. I wouldn't even consider it. After our first meeting, I signed up and went to see him for two years.

Presence

One of the hallmarks of the coaching experience is Steve's laser focus. Michael Schantz says, "I felt somehow that his strong light had singed a hole in me. For those two hours I was given his undivided attention, heartfelt listening, and unconditional support. In short, I was engulfed with love. There are very few places on this earth where that level of intimacy and trust are available." Michael signed up for one hundred hours of coaching and found that Steve brought that same vigor to each and every coaching session.

Lisa Berkovitz had a similar experience. "He is so present it feels like there is literally no one else on the planet. He said, 'So tell me everything. Who are you?' I started to tell him my story and he was fascinated. He was alive and present, with those piercing eyes."

Tom McGovern says, "There is that feeling that people talk about, the feeling that you're the only one in the room. All that is true. All his attention was focused on me. He was one hundred percent committed to me. That's quite a feeling."

This intense focus goes both ways. For Steve, it is his way of being. For his clients, it is their way to suck the marrow out of their sessions. Teresa Walding says, "It goes fast. Two hours is like a blink and you're done. You want to take in every single moment of it." John Patrick Morgan explains, "Steve doesn't allow anyone to record a session. I hate it and I love it. I wish that I had the recordings and I love that I don't because it demanded a presence of me that had me get so much more out of the work when we were together."

Clients can take notes, but it's optional. Steve is very clear that the most important thing going on is the experience. It is about having a shift in being that changes how the client sees and then acts in the world. It is not about consulting notes and remembering what Steve said. Clients get that, in time. At the beginning of their coaching, about seventy percent of Steve's clients take notes. At the end of their coaching, only ten percent do.

Tom McGovern lost the notebook that contained the majority of his notes from his two years of coaching with Steve. It was okay. "What I was left with is life is about who you're being, not what you're doing. If I am getting off track, I go back to 'Who am I being in this situation?' or 'Who do I need to be in this situation?' I can be anybody I need to be. I am not a fixed identity. That is one of the most valuable things I got from my coaching."

The Heart of the Matter

"Steve has a very unique ability to get right to the heart of the issue," says Scott Parker. That is well and good when Steve is working with your spouse or your friend or your business partner. When it is your heart and your issue, it can be disconcerting, especially when you experience the speed with which he can do it. Steve Chandler says, "For an average coach, or even a good coach, it takes a year or two to really uncover your client's limiting beliefs, because clients don't reveal them very easily. They're insecure about them to begin with. But Hardison sees them immediately." That is why Scott Parker says, "You can't bullshit Steve to save your life. You might think you are, but you're not."

Steve has no problem calling someone on their stuff, as Dr. Carla Rotering found out. She says:

Steve knows if you're getting slippery. I had something happen with my partner in my medical practice. My partner had done something that was actually pretty unethical. I was terrified of confronting him. I'm not sure why because I am the one who founded the practice, but there was something that was creating a lot of fear for me about confronting him with this. I made an agreement with Steve that I would talk to him.

In my very first session with Steve, he had said, "Look, I keep agreements. I expect you to keep agreements. If the Queen of England called and said, 'I want to see you at 11:00 on Thursday morning,' I would say to her, 'Sorry, I have a commitment with Carla.'"

So, I made this agreement with Steve that I would talk to my partner. I went back to my next session and Steve said, "How did the conversation go?"

I said, "I couldn't figure out a time to sit down with him. I was so busy. So, I sent him this letter instead."

Steve leaned over and looked at me and said, "That is not the truth." Of course, it wasn't the truth. It absolutely wasn't the truth. We worked in the same office. We worked in the same hospital. We were partners. But all my excuses felt very real to me until that moment when he said, "That is not the truth."

Self-Discovery

Diving deep into the essence of a person's being often goes deeper than his or her awareness. Gary Gietz, one of Steve's early clients, writes:

The most profound gift Steve gave me was to shine a light on a way of being that had formed everything about me since childhood. The crazy thing is that I didn't even know it was there.

Wanting people to think highly of me secretly drove every part of who I was, what I did, and the daily choices I made. It caused me to place acceptance over integrity, appearance over substance, and illusion over authenticity. It ran everything. I didn't even know it existed until Steve woke me up. He allowed me to see it and choose another way of being. We created a new game, one that I could actually win.

When signing up to work with Steve, self-discovery is always on the agenda. Rich Litvin recalls his experience:

Before I began working with Steve, I got clear that I didn't want to spend a year working on how to create more money. I'll be honest. That wasn't easy. But I didn't want to pay a lot of money to my coach only to learn how to make it back.

So Steve coached me around the deepest stuff—why I've lacked confidence for so much of my life, why I struggled around money no matter how much I earned, why I had a constant need for approval, why I couldn't even hear people's acknowledgments, why I showed up as powerless, why I was afraid to be a leader.

Openness

"You know that Steve's human, right?" said Carla Rotering. "It's foolish to think that Steve has been spared the experience of being human. It would be a mistake to believe that he hasn't bumped into hard times and grief and loss and pain and sorrow and fear and suffering and all of the things that contribute to what it is to be on the planet as a human being. What is extraordinary is that he doesn't hide that experience from anyone."

In *Creating Great Relationships*, Steve Chandler writes:

When I first started working with Steve Hardison, I remember trying to get up the courage to tell him about some of the messes I had made of my life during my younger days when I was drinking and causing trouble everywhere I went.

He could see that it was hard for me to talk about these things, so he stopped me.

"Okay, I understand. Is it okay if I talk about something else for a minute?" he asked.

"Sure," I said, glad to be changing the subject.

And then Steve launched into a series of stories that stood my hair on end. Stories from his own life about ways he had strayed from the straight and narrow as a wild youth. I was stunned. Because here he was, a business consultant, impeccably dressed and respected by top CEOs across the world, and he was describing a past that sounded like the script to *Rebel Without A Cause*. By the time he was finished, I was liberated! I was free to talk, and, boy, did I want to. Because here was a person who would understand.

"There isn't anything you could tell me about yourself that would cause me to think poorly of you," Steve laughed. "There isn't anything you've ever done or thought about doing that would ever reduce my commitment to you, my love for you, and my promise to help you become as great as you can be. Nothing would shock me. Nothing would be a negative to me. Ever."

And it was at that moment that I opened up and became more or less teachable.

Extreme Coaching

"It is very relaxing to be with Steve Chandler," says Daniel Harner. "He is like the wise grandfather that is mellow and laid back. He's very wise. He's slow and deliberate and communicates with such delicate and skillful expression. I wouldn't call being with Steve Hardison relaxing. His mind works so fast. It's very energizing, but you are also aware that you might just get your head cut off—in a loving way."

Billy Woodmansee put it this way, "Steve Hardison is a lot like a wolverine, which is, pound for pound, one of the most ferocious animals on the planet."

What happens when you take a wolverine and put him in a cage—or an office? Ask Daniel Harner. "Steve's coaching is not just formal, professional dialogue. He gets animated. He walks around. He paces. He screams, not at me, but just out there, at his bookshelf or the universe. You feel, 'Okay, he's stepping into his energy right now and it's really strong.' And then he sits down, and we keep talking."

No doubt Steve generates an energy field—and sometimes it is high voltage. That doesn't work for some people. Others thrive. John Patrick Morgan says, "Intensity is familiar to me. I can relate to it. When Steve got fired up and started shouting, I had no fear. My mom's family is Italian and my holidays are everybody yelling at each other, so I thought it was fun."

It was more than fun. In the middle of one experience, when Steve's yelling hit high decibels, John Patrick thought, "I don't think I've ever felt this loved or cared for. It was an awesome experience."

Carla Rotering says, "I have witnessed Steve's fierceness. I've not experienced it personally with him. I've never had that. I've also never had a fear of that. If I encountered Steve with that fierceness, it would absolutely call me. It would absolutely draw me forward into the flame, because fire is not a bad thing!"

Sacred Moments

Steve is a whirlwind of passion and power. He is brash, bold, and big. But underneath all that power and energy lies a tender heart. He falls in love with every client. He is deeply moved by their magnificence and courage. His awe triggers tears. The trust, the love, the baring of souls, and the shared commitment all work together to create transcendent moments. Carla Rotering shares one of hers:

I remember a time when the depth of my work with Steve had gone beyond what I had ever anticipated. Such moments are holy. Ordinary moments with Steve can also be holy, but there are some very profound moments. And the truth is, I don't really recall what this one was about. But I remember the words he said right before the experience. He said to me, "If you could see how close you are. All you have to do is tilt forward an immeasurable amount, and you would be there, because you're already there."

And then he put this music on. He got out of his chair and he held my hands and he knelt in front of me. And he wept for the whole duration of this piece of music by Kirtana. That was one of the most profound experiences of my life because of the level of connection, sacredness, and love.

The Post Game

People process their experiences with Steve differently. John Patrick Morgan shares his method:

Steve wouldn't let me record the sessions, so I scribbled as many notes as I could. When I left his office, I went to the airport. I made sure I was a couple of hours early for my flight. I used that time to type up my written notes, remembering as much as I could. Then I expanded them. On the flight home, I added more.

The next morning, I read my notes. I tidied them up. I rearranged them. And I added more. I tried to remember the stories. My few pages of written notes became twenty pages of typed notes.

Throughout the next week or two, I read my notes every morning. I was getting them into me. I took all the exercises that Steve asked me to do and all the challenges he gave me and put them on a list. I worked the list. I did the work.

Jason Jaggard involved his company in his post-game. He says:

There are about thirty-six people in our firm on three different continents. We have a Wednesday morning meeting. Often, after a session with Steve, the whole focus of that meeting was me talking about my experience. What did I learn? What did I see him do? What am I seeing now? It was like story time with Jason, as if I had gone away to a faraway land and I came back with Asian spices. And they were excited to hear. Coaches all over the world gathered to hear me tell stories about working with Steve.

After you work with Steve, there is this radioactive glow. Sometimes people really loved being with me post-Steve, and sometimes they really hated it. I came out of my session like a bat out of hell. I came out more decisive and raising the bar. It was like Red Bull.

I have often been in meetings when people said, "What's gotten into Jason?" Someone would say, "He had Steve yesterday" or "He is having a Steve day." I always created results on those days, but it was sometimes an adjustment for the people in my life.

It's not unusual for a client to walk away from Steve's office a bit dazed, wondering, "Who is this guy?" Jaya Lalita relates, "I had an enthralling two hours. It felt like I had just made a pilgrimage to this sage in the desert. And nope, I did not see him as a sage before that meeting. It was the content, the heightened quality of our time together, the import of those two hours, and all that I walked away with."

John Patrick Morgan says, "I left his office walking on a cloud, feeling so confident in myself, so happy, so peaceful, so certain." Gary Mahler relates, "The thing my wife loves about my work with Steve is every time I come home, something is different. I'm not the same. I am more loving, more kind."

Daniel Harner says, "It is going to take the rest of my life to unpack everything I have learned while coaching with Steve." For some, the rest of their life isn't long enough. Dave Orton reflects, "It was an amazing experience over which I have not gotten, over which I will never get."

Through Steve's Eyes

When asked, "If I spend the day with you, how would my life be different?" Steve responded:

For starters, you would experience aspects of yourself that prior to our meeting you were unaware of.

You would feel heard in a way that you may have never felt heard before.

You would see things that you had never seen before, about you, your life, others, their lives, and life itself.

You would feel a sense of immense love and gratitude for yourself and for me.

You would experience the distinction "presence," yours and mine.

You would want to spend another day together.

As you walked away and got in your car and drove home or flew home, you would think, and rethink, and ponder on what it is we created together, and you would say, "What happened? How did it happen? How can I keep that alive in my life?"

Loving you. Be Blessed. SFH.

Steve, 2013

Chapter 19

The Sky's the Limit

In *Through the Looking Glass*, Lewis Carroll's sequel to *Alice in Wonderland*, Alice insists a person can't believe impossible things. The queen responds, "I daresay you haven't had much practice. When I was your age, I always did it for half an hour a day. Why, sometimes I've believed as many as six impossible things before breakfast." Steve eats impossible things for breakfast, lunch, and dinner. He breathes impossible things. He swims in impossible water. None of it looks impossible. Melanie Waite says, "Steve says, 'Tell me what you want, and we will get it. We will create it. I don't care what it is.'"

Impossible thinking is not on everyone's daily diet. Instead, children often hear things like: "Money doesn't grow on trees" or "This is my shy child" or "Some things never change." Children (and adults) may say to themselves, "That's just the way I am," or

"I'm not good at math," or "I'm impatient."

Steve is crystal clear on this. We create our reality by the thoughts we think and the thoughts we buy into. So why not think something more useful, like "The sky's the limit"?

Nicholas Smith remembers sitting in the parking lot outside of a church-run commodity resource center. He and his wife had just picked up groceries because they couldn't afford to buy them. Nicholas relates:

> I got on the phone with Steve, and he spoke to me in a way no other human has ever spoken to me. Even now, I get emotional as I think about it. I asked him, "Can you—"
>
> He said yes before I finished the question.
>
> I asked, "How can you say yes if you don't even know what I'm going to ask?"
>
> "There is nothing you can ask that's bigger than me."
>
> That response impacted me. It became the foundation of my book, *The Giants and the Smalls*.

When Carla Rotering sat in Steve's office, she mentioned that she had just read something by Bruce Lipton, a stem cell biologist and the author of the bestselling book *The Biology of Belief*. He is the recipient of the 2009 Goi Peace Award. Carla mentioned to Steve that she had incredible respect for Bruce Lipton. Steve responded, "So let's call him up."

"What?" said Carla. Someone that famous? Someone that busy? Someone that important? Isn't talking to your hero a little bit scary? Even intimidating?

The next thing Carla knew, Steve had Bruce Lipton on the phone and Steve was handing the phone to her. Carla thanked Bruce for his book and his work and then handed the phone back to Steve. Steve thanked him for taking his call and for making Carla's day.

"So, that's that," said Steve. "Now you've talked to Bruce Lipton." Nothing about connecting with Bruce Lipton looked insurmountable, or even difficult, to Steve. It was just a set of actions to take, like picking up a gallon of milk at the grocery store.

When Steve served his mission in London at nineteen, one of his companions was Paul Waite. They baptized the Dixon family. At the time, Melanie Dixon was eight years old. Fast forward twenty-four years. Both Paul and Melanie were single. Steve told Melanie that she and Paul were perfect for each other.

Melanie wasn't sure. "Paul was twelve years older than I. He was divorced. He had four kids. We lived in different countries."

Steve's response was: "And . . ."

Melanie was used to thinking outside the box. She got her degree in education, but when she realized teaching wasn't for her, she left a secure profession and became an entrepreneur. She created businesses. She saw possibilities. But Steve took her to the next level of no-limit thinking. Paul and Melanie were married in 2005. Steve performed the ceremony.

Steve also revamped Michael Neill's thinking about limits and possibility. Michael writes:

On the first day of our coaching together in 2009, I was going through my goals for the year with Steve and I got to the seventh item on my list. I hesitated when I saw it.

"Well, I was going to say, 'Make over a million dollars in my business,' but I put that on the list every year so we can just ignore that one."

While he didn't say anything out loud, I noticed his left eyebrow arch as if to say, "We can leave it off the list if you like, but it would be just as easy to create it."

Somehow that raised eyebrow did more for me than any piece of coaching I could imagine. The legendary Steve Hardison didn't think it was silly or stupid or childish for me to make a million dollars. Maybe not having done it for so many years in the past didn't mean it couldn't happen this year. Maybe it didn't mean I was a bad person to want it.

Maybe, just maybe, it was really possible.

We crossed the million-dollar income threshold just over eleven months later.

Steve's attitude is contagious. Clate Mask notes, "Steve doesn't have any limits on what's possible, so he changes the way you think about limits. I don't know anybody that sees possibility like he sees possibility. He just sees stuff, and you can't help but start to see possibility when you work with him."

Billy Woodmansee says of being with Steve, "It was like he jumped inside of me and saw the part of me I don't show anyone. Then he put up a mirror and showed me how these things limit me."

Brandon Sulser is a survivor of four different traumas: a brain injury, a broken neck, freezing to death (and being revived), and a head-on auto collision. He has a master's degree in social work. He is also paralyzed from the waist down and author of the book *We Are All Paralyzed*. Brandon says, "Steve loves you more than you, at times, love yourself. He sees more in you than you see in yourself. With me, he saw the future I always wanted, but never thought I could achieve."

John Vehr says, "The reason I keep coming back to Steve is because he keeps helping me see new possibilities for how I can live my life."

Steve sees impossible futures, at least six before breakfast. He eats impossible things for breakfast, lunch, and dinner.

And he invites you to the table.

Chapter 20

Listening

Tom McGovern is a commercial real estate broker in California. He worked with Steve from 2010-2012. He reflects:

People work with Steve for different reasons. I sense this almost spiritual following that is around Steve. I don't have that so much. I'm a business guy. I went to Steve because I wanted to get some results. What I like is he walks the walk and talks the talk. It's pretty impressive.

There are a lot of people who hold themselves out to be business coaches and they are struggling to make $100,000 a year. Now, to me, that's kind of BS. How can somebody coach you to make a $1,000,000 a year if all they have been able to do themselves is make $100,000? But Steve, he's the real deal. He's doing it, and he has a background of running a company and the whole bit.

I asked him during one session, "Okay, what makes you

special? What makes you worth $5,000 dollars an hour when most coaches are $100 an hour?"

He said, "I am a master at listening."

That is definitely true. It is what I experienced. He creates a space to listen that is unmatched by anybody in the world.

Steve listens intensely. He listens with laser focus. He listens to what is said between the words and in the silences. He listens to what is not said. He listens in a way that people ask, "How do you know that? Did you call my mother?"

"At the beginning of any *Be With* session," says Steve, "I talk to my clients. I might ask them to tell me who they are, what brought them to me, or what they want to get out of our time together. Within fifteen minutes I know enough that I could work with them for a year."

The client doesn't think he has bared his soul. He has simply talked. He is shocked that Steve has discerned so much. Steve is shocked that people think that when they speak, it's just words.

"Listening" is the simplest way to describe what Steve is doing when he sits with a client. But "listening" doesn't fully capture it. Steve is also taking in visual cues, asking precise questions, and sensing what is going on. Using all his senses, Steve listens holistically. He can even listen to a picture.

Oren Harris has never met Steve in person. Their encounters are limited to a couple of phone calls, a few texts, and an internet connection. Oren relates:

We first connected when he saw my picture. He commented

on the picture, describing my essence in a way that was so precise and so clear that I felt instantly seen. He wrote, "Oren—spiritual fusion, incarnate swag, and perfect, brilliant stillness." It's like he saw into my deepest, most inner place, and then expressed it in a way that was beyond what I could articulate. I thought, "I know this soul and this soul knows me. He's seeing beyond the physical."

How does Steve do it? "Just as a person has a voice print, a fingerprint, and a specific DNA structure, they have a unique way in which they view the world. I access that," says Steve.

But *how* does he do that? Steve was born with acute senses. It's a family thing. Steve's mom had it. Steve's kids have it. Amy doesn't. It's an intensity thing. It's also about being totally present, with no distractions—no thoughts of last night's date, tonight's basketball game, or what you are going to say next.

Experience is also a factor. With every conversation, Steve hones his listening. With each year, this ability gains momentum and speed, so much so that even Steve is surprised at how quickly he knows what is going on inside a person.

There is something else, something more elusive. When asked to explain how he listens, Steve says, "It is seeing, feeling, hearing, and also something else I can't put into words. I am a huge receptor." Iyanla says, "Steve hears, not with his ears, but with his being."

Several years and a few thousand books ago, Amy read an account of a woman who had been deaf since birth. As a child, she thought her mother had special powers. Every time her mother opened the door, someone appeared. When the girl opened the door, no one was there. It was many years before she understood that her mother heard the doorbell ring. She did not.

In trying to describe what gives Steve the ability to listen the way he docs, perhaps we should simply say that Steve hears the doorbell; most people do not.

Chapter 21

Creation

Steve likes his cars. And he likes his personalized license plates. He is intentional in choosing just the right word for his license plate, one that captures who he is or what he is currently focusing on. He tinkers with the seven allotted spaces. He plays with the possibilities. Finally, he chooses his favorite. After a couple of years, he starts the process again. He likes change. But he is also nostalgic. He keeps his old license plates on a wall in his garage. A partial list includes:

MASTERY   AMYSGUY

LTGO2LV   INOVATE

SFH   COACHIN

BEBLSSED   LUVINGU

He wanted CREATE, but it was taken. He came up with CR8IVE. It describes Steve well. He zigs when others zag, creating ways to get things done that are so far out of the box that the box is a speck in the rearview mirror. He creates possibilities for his clients that are non-linear. He creates space for people to step into their magnificence. He creates his life. It's a good license plate for him.

Creation in Coaching

"My office is a place of pure creation," says Steve. Steve Chandler agrees. "I would bring a problem from my life to our coaching session. Steve would never say, 'How are we going to solve this?' or 'How do you want to communicate with your creditor?' or 'How do you want to repair that relationship?' He would say, 'Given this situation, what do you want to create?'"

Carla Rotering says:

Steve always said to me, "So given this, what do you want to create? . . . And *now* what do you want to create? . . . And *now* what do you want to create?" That is the world according to Hardison, right? He takes things that don't exist and makes them exist.

My dream was to create a home on Anguilla, a Caribbean island that I was in love with. I had absolutely no idea how to do that. No idea. I'm a fifty-year-old single woman who practices medicine ninety hours a week. Steve helped me turn that dream into reality. In the time I coached with Steve, I actually purchased a piece of land on Anguilla and started building the house.

I now have this beautiful, 4500 square foot house in the Caribbean. I have had it for twenty years.

Taking things that don't exist and making them exist is second nature to Steve. John Patrick Morgan says, "One of Steve's clients once said Steve has pathological certainty. I love that. Pathological certainty. He has absolute certainty that everything that you speak can and will be created." It doesn't look so simple to the rest of us. There are practical realities we have to work with, right?

Karan Rai relates his experience:

We had sessions where Steve would say, "What do you want to talk about?" If I didn't have anything specific, he would say, "Well, let's just be present." We would sit in meditation and then we would go with whatever came up for me.

And then there were sessions where I went in knowing I needed a complete strategy. At one coaching session, I was in the middle of a deal and my backers fell out. I had to raise seventy or eighty million bucks to get the deal closed.

Steve casually said, "Okay, well, let's create some new backers."

"Steve, that's not how it works in the real world. You can't just create new backers."

"Of course you can," he said. "That's exactly how it works."

And we did.

One of the things that clients *must* create if they are going to work with Steve is that their time together in the most important thing in their world. It's not an ego thing. Steve explains:

There are things that are urgent, critical, or important, but they aren't sitting there like that. They must be *created* as urgent, critical, or important.

When I meet with my clients, we deal with their lives—

identity, their relationships, their future—everything. If they let something that important get bumped off by a board meeting or a last-minute invitation to golf at a premier resort, they aren't ready to work with me. I will give them my life and my blood, but they have to match my commitment. If they do, there is no end to the miracles we can create.

Creating Being

"For Steve, creativity doesn't belong solely to certain fields like music and art," says Steve Chandler, "but to everything, and especially to being. He creates who he wants to be in the world and then lives from that creation. He taught me that creation in being is possible for anyone."

Steve begins creating who he is the moment he wakes up. It is the last thing he does before he goes to sleep. And he does it in every conversation and every thought. Constant creation. He speaks who he is loudly and boldly everywhere he goes. The person he creates himself to be is also big and bold. His personal declaration begins, "I am the universe."

He has been accused of arrogance, but it isn't arrogance to Steve. Every time he declares who he is, Steve is creating himself to himself, to others, and to the universe. Every time he creates himself, he is making it more real. The idea of a person burying his magnificence is offensive to Steve. He believes false humility is pernicious. He refuses to go there.

When asked about creation, Steve said this:

With every question, with every answer, with every conversation, I am creating. It's all I do all day long. Actually, it is all you do all day long too. You cannot not create. But what I am talking about is consciously choosing what you create through your thinking and speaking.

I love to create possibility. I create possibility with my clients. I create possibility with people who want to put their voice into the world. I create possibility with the people who contact me because they are at the end of their rope.

The most important creation of all is creating oneself. People do so many things to prop up their image to the outside world. They make money. They buy big homes and expensive cars. They get advanced degrees. They work out to get the perfect body. There is nothing wrong with these things. The problem comes when people use them to compensate for something missing in their being. Too often, people use them to tell the world how they want to be seen.

The better option is to create your being. If a person knows at his core (in other words, in his being), "I am valuable. I am important. I am beautiful," then the outer trappings are optional. You can have them or not have them and be okay with yourself. If you do have them, you can enjoy them. Being is an inside job. There is no part of being that is external.

Being is also a constant choice. If I have an interaction that doesn't work, I need to ask myself, "Who was I being?" I probably slipped out of my created way of being. I was still creating my being. It just wasn't a useful one. As soon as I am aware of it, I can choose to create something more useful.

The only way someone can shift their being is to see it and shift it. Someone else can't shift it. A book can't shift it. An inspiring TED Talk can't shift it. A great coach can't shift it. A book, a talk, and a coach can help you see it. But *you* have to see it and *you* have to choose to shift it. You are the creator of your being.

In 2016, Steve created a way for people to experience him without a fifty-hour or one-hundred-hour agreement. It isn't a coaching session, but it is a committed space and a committed time where people get to be with Steve in an intimate conversation about their being. They get to see Steve's way of being. They get to see their own way of being. Not surprisingly, Steve calls it a "Be With Session."

Creating Others

Creation is the heart of Steve's coaching, but he doesn't only create with clients. Because it is his way of being, it spills out on family, friends, and even strangers.

Cherryl Vernon, Amy's niece, writes:

Over twenty years ago, when I was a young adult, I asked Steve what he did for a living. He sat me down at a table and started talking to me. He asked me questions and he listened intensely to my answers. It wasn't a very long conversation, but I will always remember it because he told me that I was a genius. I could tell he really meant it.

Knowing what a successful person he was, it affected me. How could it not increase your confidence and self-esteem to know someone thinks so highly of you? Steve sees people's potential and strengths and builds people up so that they see those things in themselves.

Cherryl and her husband Bruce, a veterinarian, are the owners of Market Street Pet Depot, a pet store that offers veterinarian services, pet grooming, dog training, and a pet hospital. Cherryl employed her gifts to design a store that feels a little like Disneyland's Main Street, with each department having its own unique storefront and ambience. Her innovative design has won awards.

Steve met Jered Schager when Jered was the general manager of the Porsche dealership in Chandler, Arizona. Jered says:

> Steve had an issue with the clear bra on his Porsche. We took care of it. When he came and picked the vehicle up, he had me take him to the back to where our detailers and the clear bra guys are so he could thank them.
>
> I've been in the car business twenty-six years, and that had never happened. Those guys are one of the more underappreciated positions in the business. I know. I started my career in their position. For a customer to go back there and thank them . . . Well, they were floored.

Steve routinely thanks the cooks at restaurants and the housekeeping staff at hotels. But he doesn't just thank. He creates. Steve lets them know that their work is valued and that they are important. When Steve walks away, people are smiling and standing a little bit taller.

Steve helps every client create a deliberately chosen and powerful way of being. Every client discards ways of being that do not serve him.

Ward Andrews recounts his experience:

> I came from very little. There was no one giving me money. I had to earn everything. There was a point earlier in my life where I was down to a few hundred dollars. I had a mortgage and kids, and I didn't have a job. Experiences like that have

a way of lingering. So, I can be very frugal. It is where I naturally come from.

I've been successful, so I don't *need* to be so frugal, but it was hard to break old habits. One time I showed Steve a picture of my trash can outside my house. It was overflowing with trash, piles upon piles of trash. I told him that I needed to get a second trash can. He agreed. But it cost five dollars more a month. My mindset was such that I didn't want to pay for the extra trash can.

Steve worked with me on my scarcity mentality. I remember him telling me that I was the poorest wealthy guy he had ever sat with. I was a pauper—not on paper, but in my head. He helped me come from abundance.

How does Steve teach his clients to create their lives? It all begins with the document.

Chapter 22

The Document

Erin Donovan walked out of Steve's office after her first official coaching session. She had a new identity. As Steve walked her out to her car, Dustin Venekamp happened to drive by. Dustin is Steve's neighbor and also a client. Dustin stopped to say hi. Steve said, "Dustin, let me introduce you to Erin. She has the smile of the universe."

"Hi. I'm Dustin. I exist to serve."

At some point in their work together, Steve helps every client create a deliberately chosen, powerful way of being. It is a significant part of the creation that goes on in his office. It is so significant that it becomes part of a client's identity. It is so significant that Daniel Harner says, "It is the whole experience with Steve. It is the ultimate empowerment. If you have that, you have access to everything."

Creating a new way of being begins by creating a list of declarations that are collectively known by Steve and his clients as "the document." Some clients refer to them as their "declarations" or their "I am statements." The statements in the document manifest the highest, noblest essence of who you are. They are you at your inner core, you without baggage, you without wounds, damage, or fear. They are you without the need to impress or the struggle to be good enough. They are the you you know you are in your gut when you have moments of clarity. They are the you that soars.

These statements are not goals or affirmations. Goals are great. Affirmations are powerful—as far as they go. But too often, goals and affirmations are short-sheeted by underlying beliefs. For instance, one of Steve's male clients had the underlying belief that "women are a pain in the butt." It is challenging to build a good relationship on top of that. Another client had an underlying thought, "I'm not respected. I am always dismissed." When that is your dominant thought, it is hard to step into your power.

Creating goals and affirmations without first examining your underlying beliefs is what Steve calls "putting frosting on dog poop." That is why creating a new way of being begins with digging deep and doing internal work.

John Vehr says, "Since I was nineteen years old, I have known how to talk to myself to create a future that is awesome, but I didn't pay attention to the thoughts that are below the surface, the thoughts that *really* run me. I didn't know how to access those."

Most people are unaware of the thoughts that determine their lives. These thoughts exist like water to a fish. But just because you are unaware of them, it doesn't mean you aren't wet. So, Steve's first assignment when you create your document is to notice the thoughts you currently have about yourself and your world.

John describes his experience:

> In one of our coaching sessions, Steve mentioned this amazing woman he had worked with. I told him I would like to meet her. Steve didn't respond, so I said more forcefully, "Steve, I would really, *really* like to meet her."
>
> Steve looked at me and said, "Uh . . . no." At the time, I was a womanizer. Later I could see that he was protecting her from me. That night, I was thinking about her and a thought came to me, "Why would a woman like that be with a guy like you?" I was shocked. Where did that come from? That's not how I talked to myself. Once I zeroed in on that thought, I started hearing all kinds of thoughts that didn't serve me at all. I saw the spin I was putting on my life, and it was covering up the mess that was down below.
>
> I spent about six weeks getting all these thoughts on paper. Then Steve said, "You have written enough down. Let's create a new reality."
>
> "So, I just take 'I'm not powerful' and turn it into 'I'm powerful'?"
>
> Steve laughed. "It's not that easy. Your ego is too powerful to be tricked. We can't just put a positive thought on top of a negative one. It would be like putting a crown on a tooth without getting rid of the underlying decay. You have to exercise radical self-forgiveness on those judgments. Once you do, you are in a clear world. Then you create your declarations."

Steve taught John to forgive himself. Self-forgiveness is easy in theory, but it's hard to actually do. For some, beating yourself up feels more appropriate than self-forgiveness. But it hurts. Steve has created a process for self-forgiveness that is accessible and effective. He is hesitant to describe it, lest the reader turn it into a formula and dilute it. The reader must remember that when Steve works with his clients, so much of the power comes from being present in the moment, knowing where to go and what to say based on what the client has just said.

By analogy, the explanation of the self-forgiveness process is like a tiger in the zoo. The intuitive, in-the-moment coaching is like a tiger in the wild. One is more accessible. The other has raw power that sends shivers down your spine. The tigers in this book are at the zoo.

Self-Forgiveness

Steve's first step in teaching self-forgiveness is to distinguish the concept "self." When Steve refers to "self," he is speaking of the inner voice that delivers a running commentary about you and your life. It is this internal monologue that determines how you see yourself. For instance, if you drop something and break it, your self might say, "You are so clumsy." Or it might say, "Accidents happen." The self has an opinion about everything. It is constantly judging whether you are brilliant or stupid, bold or afraid, good enough or inadequate.

Once a client understands the concept of self, Steve asks him to identify and write down the things the self says. These things are actually self-judgments. Steve explains, "It doesn't matter if some-one else—parent, teacher, or sibling—originally said these things to you. If you didn't buy into them, they would not have adhered. *You* glued them into your self-concept. *You* made them true."

The next step is self-forgiveness. Steve helps his clients understand self-forgiveness with metaphors. One metaphor is that the mind is the consummate GPS. With a traditional GPS, if you type in "1010 Arthur Street," it takes you to 1010 Arthur Street. If you type in "Disneyland," it takes you to Disneyland. Occasionally, there is a fail, but GPSs are exceptionally accurate. Your mind is flawless. If you input "I'm amazing," you get amazing. If you input "I'm afraid," you get fear. If you input "I have extraordinary decision-making abilities," that is what you get. Most people have plenty of crippling thoughts stored in their personal GPS. However, they are not etched in stone.

Another metaphor Steve uses comes from the world of word processing. The find-and-replace feature in word processing apps allows you to find every occurrence of a specific word and replace it with a different word in seconds, no matter how long your document. The mind has the same amazing ability to replace a destructive thought with an empowering one. Every time you catch yourself judging yourself, you can replace it with "I forgive myself for judging myself as . . ."

John Vehr mastered self-forgiveness, which brought him to a place of ultimate clarity. From there, his declarations emerged. John relates, "'I'm not powerful' became 'I am an extension of the one true God and I am powerful beyond measure.' But I didn't create that. I don't talk like that. It came through me." Tapping into the Divine, "I was able to create a manifesto that is truer than who I was being."

Norma Bachoura describes her experience:

I take a lot of Christian courses, especially on how to help people through prayers and through declarations. People say you need to declare, "I am a child of God. I'm loved by God. I'm this. I'm that." But these declarations never worked when I did them. It felt like I was lying to myself. I could never figure out why they didn't work.

In my first session with Steve, he helped me write down all the negative thoughts I told myself about myself. I forgave myself, and then I spoke the truth. Those declarations worked like a charm because they were born out of me. In about two to three weeks, the thoughts that had played like a broken record—devastating thoughts like "you're ugly"—no longer existed.

In about two months, what naturally came into my brain was, "You're loved by God. God is going to take care of you. You're such a beautiful woman. You're very smart. You can do anything that you set your mind to." These thoughts popped up automatically. Before, I could never figure out how to change the negative record in my brain to a positive record.

This inner work, rigorously done, is essential. Marina Lazaris learned that firsthand. She was impressed with Steve's document and wanted to have one of her own. After she created her document, she shared it with Steve. When he read it, he was stunned. It was his document, with a few tweaks. He called her.

"Marina, you can't take my statements and start using them like they are your own. It won't work. You have to do the work that generated them. I created 'I am extraordinarily patient, loving, and kind to all living things, especially to Amy Blake Hardison' because I wasn't always nice to my wife. I wasn't always loving. It took soul-searching and forgiveness, from myself and Amy. That statement is my prayer."

Marina got it. She created a document based on her life and her vision.

Shout It Out

Once a client has identified his self-judgments, forgiven himself, and created his document, Steve has him commit the document to memory.

Steve encourages—even pushes—his clients to speak their documents loudly, frequently, and boldly. That begins with speaking your document every morning and every night. Why? Because what creates your reality is what you think about and what you talk about each day. Simple enough. But for some, the gap between the document and current reality is disconcerting.

Daniel Harner says, "Saying some of those statements is uncomfortable for me. Steve will say, 'Just say it twenty-five times. It doesn't matter how you feel, or how much you don't believe it. Just do it. The doing of it will create it.'"

It is well to remember that the document faces forward, not backward. It is not a report on the past but a future to live into. As Dave Orton says, "This is a living document. It is possibility. I am not the fulfilment of these things yet. It's where I come from."

When it comes to saying your document, there is speaking and there is *speaking*. If you want your document to have the power of transformation, you energize it. Steve says, "When I say, 'I am the universe,' I am going into my mind and picturing the universe. I see it expanding. I have a visceral connection with the expansion. Like the universe, I am constantly expanding who I am, what I know, and what I see. I am the universe. I dance with my document. I feel it. I experience it."

In September 2017, Steve and fourteen of his clients attended a Byron Katie event at Big Sur, California. Their attendance fee included meals at a cafeteria on site. During one break, Steve and his clients gathered at the cafeteria. Many of these clients knew about each other but had never met. Karan Rai suggested each person share who they were. Each spoke their document.

Afterwards, a stranger approached Steve and said, "Wow, I only heard part of that, but what I heard was amazing. Who are you?"

"Do you want to know my name or who I am?" asked Steve. She wanted the latter. Steve stood inches from her. "I am the universe. Love is. I am That . . ."[1]

Flowing in your Blood

Speaking your document to yourself and to others is essential, but it is just the beginning. Daniel Harner says, "Steve wants you to be the embodiment of your document. It is to be so much a part of you that it is second nature, like muscle memory. Steve says, 'If I cut your arm open, I want to see your document flowing in your blood.'" It is no surprise that Steve has little patience for those clients who are casual about their document, as A.J. Richards found out. He relates:

> I'd been running the gym for a while when I was hired by Chris Powell from the TV show *Extreme Makeover* to be a weight-loss coach. Having worked with Steve and done many of the Landmark programs, I had started to unfold a level of consciousness and awareness that I'd never understood before. I knew that was what people needed in weight loss. The act of losing weight has everything to do with who they know themselves to be. If I believe I'm fat, I'm going to do things fat people do, right? Athletes don't stop for fast food because in their head they're an athlete,

---

[1] Steve's full document starts on page 153.

and athletes don't do that. This was the direction I wanted to go with these people.

I contacted Steve and said, "Would it be okay with you if I taught the process of forgiving yourself, not judging yourself, and creating a document?"

He said, "Why don't you come and see me?"

Now, keep in mind, I wasn't actually doing this process when I asked him. I'd dropped my twice-daily declarations after a few months. In hindsight, it wasn't a smart move.

The way I recall it, I went to his office and sat down. Steve asked one simple question: "Who are you?"

I hadn't committed my document to memory enough that I could tell him who I was. Steve turned his head to the side, and he spit on his floor.

"You asked me if you could teach what I teach and you're not even doing it. That is like spitting in my face."

And he spit on his floor again.

Steve is a father figure to me. He is beyond a father figure. I owe a big part of my life to who he is for me. When he spit on his floor, it shook me to my core. It was the wakeup call I needed.

Then he said, "Can you hear me? I love you."

That was a year ago, and I have been committed to speaking my document since then.

The Difference

What difference do the documents make in the lives of the people who have created them? The document is not magic. It is a declaration and a commitment. Daniel Harner says, "Steve encourages the speaking, being, and *doing* of your document."

Steve is crystal clear on this. He says, "You are the one

responsible to go out and make your document happen." The document pulls you into action. It invites you to step into opportunities you might have passed up pre-document. It is your partner as you dance with possibility. But you still have to dance.

Those who put on their dancing shoes find the document's impact is considerable. Jeff Dinsdale was having a bad day. He doesn't have many. He is pretty balanced. But this day, he was in a funk. He was coaching with Steve at the time and he reached out to him. He recalls, "I called and left a message. I said, 'Hey, I'm having a bad day. Do you have any advice? Blah, blah, blah . . .' I guess I was kind of dramatic about it. All he texted back was 'Read your declarations and get in action.' That was it. It was just that simple."

Karan Rai shares his experience:

I knew it was going to be damn hard. It was my first marathon. It was in Antarctica. We were running on a glacier wearing crampons. It was fifty below. I'm not a runner. I do CrossFit. I stay fairly fit, but I'm not a runner. I wasn't even halfway through the marathon and everything was hurting. I had a shin splint. It felt like I was getting frostbite on my face. I remember thinking, "What am I doing out here?"

It was at that moment that I remembered Steve saying, "When you get into a place where you start questioning yourself, just be quiet and create yourself."

I was maybe ten miles into the marathon, in the middle of a glacier, on an open track. There were only forty-two people running this race, so there was no one else around, just me and my misery.

I clearly remember getting in a zone and starting to chant my "I am" statements. They became my mantra. "I am a powerful creator and I speak my world into existence. I am an unstoppable force of nature and accomplish the improbable and the impossible with ease. . . ." That really helped me get centered and focused, and it gave me my second, third, and fourth wind.

The fact that my document came up for me was not accidental. It's in my mind. It's in my bones. It naturally comes up whenever I need it. I have used it so many times.

I'm in private equity. I'm in the business of buying companies. It's an industry with a lot of big personalities. Everybody's smarter than everybody else. There are a whole bunch of egos in the room. There have been so many times when in the middle of shit going sideways, I have excused myself and gone to the bathroom to compose myself. I literally recreated the guy that walked back into that room. And it has shifted meetings.

When you are feeling distress or you're feeling anxious, it is because you're off your center. Your document is who you truly are. When that guy shows up, everything is easy. The question is, how do you get him to show up at the right time? And I think that's what my work with Steve has given me. That's the superpower that I have gained working with him.

Abigail and Edward Olaya are parents of triplets. They are also former clients of Steve, which means they each have a document. One day, Abigail and Edward were discussing what they wanted for their daughters. If they could give them anything, what would it be? The answer was easy: the document. So together, Abigail, Edward, and their six-year-old triplets created a document. Audrey, Ava, and Adelina were not silent partners. This is what they came up with:

Audrey, Ava, and Adelina's Document

I am enough.

I am in control of my power—my thoughts, my feelings, and my actions.

I am so brave.

I have peace inside of me.

I am kind, loving, and grateful.

I am so loved.

I am loving to my family.

I am so cute.

I respect my body.

I can learn anything I want to.

I am so beautiful.

I am loving to myself.

That is a formidable foundation for six-year-olds. But do they get it? Abigail says:

It may seem like a lot for young children to grasp, but they get it. They really do. Their eyes sparkle when they say their declarations. They speak them to each other in the day, saying, "You are such a loving sister" or "You are so beautiful." And when they say their declarations, they throw in new ones based on whatever they are feeling at the moment. That is how "I am so cute" got on the list. In some ways it is easier for six-year-olds to get declarations than adults. They have far less programming to undo.

The triplets say their document once a day, sometimes in the morning, sometimes in the car. They also say it if they are struggling, if they need an energizing pick-me-up, or even if they just encounter a routine snag.

The Olayas live in a house with a split floor plan. Abigail says, "Sometimes when I ask one of the girls to go get something, she will say, 'I don't want to go to the other side of the house by myself. Can someone go with me?' I will say, 'You are so brave.' It gives them something to live into." The document gives them tools to handle things. If someone at school says they don't like their hair, "it just rolls off of them because we have our declarations. They can recognize their power. They are intentional at a very young age."

The 11:11 Masterpiece

For many years, Steve and Amy had six flourishing ficus trees in their backyard, near Steve's office. They were pretty. They were green, a highly desirable feature in Arizona, but they also dropped their leaves and berries onto the deck, into the ornamental rocks and, most annoying of all, into the pool. They did it daily. Hourly. Finally, enough was enough. Out they came. But the treeless space was harsh. Their son, Clint, dubbed it "the prison yard."

After much discussion, the idea for an extensive wall mural was born and Nadine Larder was engaged. The wall was sealed and painted with an undercoat. Before Nadine began painting, Steve had his clients write their documents on the wall.

Every day, two or three clients penned their document in black marker on the white wall. It took each client at least an hour, sometimes two, occasionally three. Sometimes they were still

writing when night fell, and Steve took out a flood light. Amy, ever the pragmatist, questioned spending all that time writing on the wall when it would be covered up in a few weeks. Steve never wondered.

From a distance, the wall looked like an enormous newspaper. Close up, it read like a manifesto to change the world. Here is a sampling, taken from several clients' declarations:

My very breath is enough. I am love. I serve all humanity.
I am a lighthouse.
I am an inspirational leader who brings out the best in others.
I am excellence personified. I am profound wisdom. I am unconditional love.
My life is contribution. I use my time and money to bless others.
I love me for who I am and I love me for whom I am not.
I am Abraham Lincoln leadership.
I live a life I love with those I love, and I love it.

I bring out the best in others.

I run towards scary things.

I am unconditional happiness.

I am consciously kind. I am deliberately patient.

I am a warrior of the heart.

I am a Christian, a family man, and a billion-dollar company CEO. I know my priorities and I enjoy the journey.

I am a powerhouse. I am that there are no problems, just solutions. I am that I take actions to produce extraordinary results. I am that people light up and are their best self when I am around. I create for my family a home full of love, understanding, and fun.

Each evening, Amy and Steve stood in front of the wall, reading the latest edition. They took in the declarations. They felt their power. They experienced the magnificence of humankind. One evening, a week before Nadine was slated to begin, Amy turned to Steve and said, "Are you sure you want to paint over them?"

Today, vibrant paintings cover six panels of the block wall. Each reflects people finding their power, illuminating their soul, and transforming their lives. The documents are still there, under the beauty.

Dozens of clients left something of their magnificence, vision, and commitment in the wall. There is power in the wall. But even more, there is power in the clients. As Karan Rai says, "When you have your document inside of you, you get to the point where you are no longer arguing with yourself for your limitations. You start arguing with yourself for your greatness. It changes how you view the world, and that by extension changes how the world interacts with you."

Nadine Larder, the artist, and Steve, 2017

Steve's Document

I am the Universe.

Love is. I am That.

Be still and know that I AM God.

I am a disciple of Jesus Christ.

I am deeply moved by Spirit, the power of all Creation.

I am consciously aware of other people's points of view and I honor their right to have a different point of view.

I am Lovingkindness.

I am that no one is worthy of my judgment and that everyone is worthy of my Love.

I am graciously authentic.

I am strong, healthy, and attractive.

I am happy and peaceful.

I am that my heart is filled with peace.

I am Divine Intuition.

I am connected to Infinite Intelligence.

I experience extraordinary discernment and decision-making powers.

I dedicate all thought to Union.

I am that I do not sweat the small stuff, and it is all small stuff, including death and dying.

I am that I have no complaints.

I distinctly remember forgetting that—and the "that" is my past. I never use my past to victimize myself or others. I do not wallow in it. I use my past to lead, build, inspire, teach and love.

I am madly in Love with my intelligent, gorgeous, brilliant and vivacious wife, Amy Blake Hardison.

I am that I am extraordinarily patient, loving, and kind to all living things, especially Amy Blake Hardison.

I am that I live, I love, I learn, and I serve, profoundly and extraordinarily.

This is who I am, and my mother named me Steve.

Chapter 23

Being Your Word, Commitment, and Integrity

Sitting in the jury assembly room with two hundred prospective jurors was pure pleasure for Steve, whose version of the quote "So many books, so little time" is "So many conversations, so little time." He met a fascinating woman. Of course, it could have been a man, a banker, an auto mechanic, a grizzled hippie, a Harley enthusiast, a transvestite, an exotic dancer, a grandma, ad infinitum. People fascinate Steve. But this time, it was a woman.

She was interested in what Steve did. He said he had a book in his car that he would give her. Steve was chosen to be on the jury; she was dismissed. She left hours before he did. Some people would say, "Oh well. That's how it goes." That's not how it goes for Steve. "Anything that comes out of my lips," says Steve, "I take action on." At the end of a long day in court, he drove an hour out of his way to deliver the book to her. Her words were predictable. "You didn't need to do this."

Steve's words were less predictable. "I needed to do it for me."

Why? Because if Steve says he is going to do something, he does it. It is his cardinal principle. He lives it. He breathes it. He has taught it to his kids. As adults, they have each said, "Do you realize that most people don't do what they say? It is so frustrating!" This is something that has always confounded Steve, ever since his father set him on the porch and told him he would take him to the mountains, and never did.

Doing what you say you will do—being your word—imparts power. Things get done. Efficiency soars. Frustration falls. It's so obvious. It is surprising how frequently people don't do what they say they will do. It is shocking how unaware people are of the discrepancy.

When Steve asks a group of people how many of them keep their word, almost everyone raises his hand. When he asks clients how often they do what they say they will do, most estimate high. Clate Mask projected ninety percent. Then Steve sent Clate off with an assignment to keep count of every time he did and didn't do what he said. When he came back to his next coaching session, Clate's estimate had plunged to twenty percent. And Clate is a high-producing, effective CEO.

Most people know only a few people they can count on like their life depends on it. How can you become one of the few? You begin by paying attention to what you say. And what if you fall short?

Steve explains, "No one is one hundred percent, but if I say something, the odds are really high that I am going to do it. If I don't, I clean it up. I speak to the person I made the agreement with, acknowledge that I didn't do what I said, and make a new agreement."

Byron Applegate says, "If you know Steve, then you know that your word is all you have, and commitment is how you know what to do next."

Commitment

Steve was picking up a few things from the grocery store when his phone rang. The caller introduced himself. We will call him William. William said, "I want you to be my coach."

"You'll have to get in line," replied Steve.

It was not the response William expected.

Steve asked William what prompted him to call. William knew one of Steve's clients. He had seen his transformation. William wanted some of that. Again, he asked Steve to be his coach, upping the ante. He would fly him to Las Vegas in his personal jet so Steve could coach him in his home. He would pay triple Steve's usual fee.

"Sorry, I can't be your coach."

"Why?"

"First of all, I only coach in my office at my house. Second, because you want to own me. I am not ownable."

William was intrigued. He committed to be in Steve's office on a specific date, at a specific time, with a check for $150,000. For Steve, it wasn't a done deal. He needed to make sure William's commitment was big enough to produce results.

When they met in his office, Steve outlined for William what he would need to commit to if they were to work together:

1. Their work together must be the most important thing in William's world, not because he was working with Steve, but because they were working on William's life.

2. He must be in Steve's office when he said he would. They would agree on their schedule at the beginning of their coaching, allowing for vacations, conferences, etc. After that, their sessions had absolute priority over things that came up.
3. He must be open to what Steve said—very likely it would not be what William wanted to hear.
4. He must be willing to learn to love.

When William hedged, Steve picked up the $150,000 check and tore it into pieces. William's jaw dropped. William was a billionaire. No one talked to him like that. No one disregarded his money like that. It got his attention. He committed. He pulled out his checkbook and started to write another check.

"And cut off your left testicle and your right pinkie finger and give them to me with your check."

William's head jerked up. Steve was smiling—but he was also serious. Not about the testicle and pinkie finger, but about the importance of commitment. For Steve, commitment is fundamental. Like being your word, it is something he works on with every client.

When Steve worked with Tom McGovern on commitment, he used an analogy that Tom has frequently shared and still uses to this day.

"Imagine you are with a group of fifty people. These are your people. It could be a church group, your local Rotary club, whatever. You ask who can help you set up chairs for a meeting next Saturday at 8:00 a.m. Ten people raise their hands. Saturday morning comes and not everybody who committed to be there at 8:00 is there. Name some reasons people might give for not showing up."

Tom threw out some conventional excuses: "I had a flat tire. I ran out of gas. I overslept. I forgot."

Steve continued, "If you were to list these reasons on the left side of a piece of ledger paper, how long would the list be? How many possibilities are there?"

"Dozens. Hundreds."

"Now," said Steve, "on the right side of the ledger paper, write how you know if someone has honored his commitment? How long is this list? How many possibilities are there?"

The list was short. There was one possibility. "He showed up at 8:00. He did what he said he would do."

Then, pointing to the right-hand side of the paper, Steve said, "That's me. That's my life. I am commitment."

Tom reflects, "I certainly get that about Steve. If he says he's going to do something, you can bank on it. It is a very, very, very powerful way of living."

Integrity

"Steve is an amazing coach," says Van Dunham. "He has the ability to identify when an individual is out of balance and out of integrity. Then he guides you back into balance and back into integrity." Sometimes "guide" isn't quite the right word. Sometimes it feels a little more like a shove. Just ask Jeff Dinsdale.

I was twenty-two years old. I was working at University of Phoenix in sales. I had just hired Steve to be my coach and my first session was at 9:00 a.m. I was supposed to be at work at 8:00.

My boss was this ex-hockey player. He was a big, macho guy, not this transformed guy. I was pretty sure that telling him I was going to meet with a life coach was not going to fly. So, I called in and let them know I would be running a

159

little bit late because my grandma had had a heart attack and was in the hospital. Why did I say that? Because no one's going to come back and try to pin you on that.

I showed up at Steve's and we started talking about what brought me there. I told him, "Man, I've done so much to get here and to have this session with you. I even told my boss this morning that my grandma's in the hospital. I was willing to do whatever it takes to be here." I didn't even realize how out of integrity I was. I was so blind to it.

Steve said, "I want to show you something." We went into his family room and he turned on the TV. He showed me a *60 Minutes* segment about Bernie Madoff, whose one little white lie led to the biggest Ponzi scheme in history. He turned to me and said, "That is what out-of-integrity behavior looks like."

When I went to my work, I said to my ex-NHL, big, manly-guy manager, "Hey, bro, can we go on a walk?" On the walk I said, "I just want to clean something up with you. My grandma wasn't in the hospital this morning. I just said that because I went to meet with this coach. And to be honest, I felt embarrassed, and I felt nervous. I didn't know what to say. And I wanted an out."

He said, "Jeff, thanks so much for sharing that. Do you know how many of the people I manage bullshit me every day about this sick person or that sick person and I know they're lying?"

So that was my first session with Steve. He smashed me over the head with integrity. That conversation changed the course of my life.

Being your word, commitment, and integrity are in the same domain. If one of them is wobbly, all three are weakened. If all three are rock solid, your life is altered—and not just a little bit. As economist Michael Jensen points out, the increase isn't negligible—"it's more like 100 to 500 per cent."[2]

No wonder these things are an essential preface for Steve's primary focus: working with a person's thoughts.

---

[2] See Michael Jensen, "Integrity: Without It Nothing Works," https://papers.ssrn.com/sol3/papers.cfm?abstract_id=1511274

Chapter 24

Steve on Thought and Action

"Other coaches deal with their clients' stuff by going outside," says Steve. "If a client says he has a problem with his wife, most coaches start working on the problem; perhaps it is communication. I go in—every single time. What creates our problems, what creates our whole lives, is our thoughts."

Going in. Working with thoughts. That is Steve's work.

The following are Steve's views regarding thoughts and action, in his own words.

Principle 1: Action

Sometimes when I am talking to clients, I will ask them what they think the most important traits are in order to create a desired outcome. The desired outcome can be in any area, from becoming a company president to losing weight to writing a screenplay.

Some people say desire. "Desire is good," I respond, "but do you know people who have desire who can't produce?" Of course they do.

Some people say passion. "Passion is important. It is better to have passion than to not have passion, but there are passionate people who have no results."

Other answers include a good college degree, perseverance, vision, belief, and attitude. These are all important, but they aren't the determining factor. Only one person, Holly Profitt-Venekamp, hit the bullseye.

The key factor to creating a desired outcome is action.

Principle 2: How We See the World

If there is one secret to life, it is this: All actions are directly correlated to how we see the world. Notice that I didn't say, "All actions are directly correlated to how the world is." The world is not a fixed reality, seen by everyone the same way. For instance, I'm color blind. For the first fifteen years of our marriage, I thought we had green plates. Eventually, I said something to Amy about the green plates. She had no idea what I was talking about. To her, they were wheat-colored. The plates looked different to me than they did to Amy. The world we experience is a personal experience, not a universal one.

To show my clients that every action is directly correlated to how they see the world, I pick up a pillow from the couch and start to hit them. Inevitably, they hold up their arms to deflect the pillow. I point out that if we were having a quiet conversation, they wouldn't throw their arms up into the air all of a sudden. That would be crazy. Only when they perceive a reason to put their arms up in the air do they raise their arms.

I say to my clients, "Notice, right now you are just sitting here. You aren't dropping to the floor and crawling to the corner of the room. That would be bizarre. But if a bullet came through the window, that is exactly what you would do, and it would make perfect sense." Every single behavior we take is based on how we see the world.

In one coaching session, Clate Mask [the CEO of Keap] and I were talking about his company's sales. I told him that his top salesperson and his lowest-producing salesperson are not taking the same actions. If he could get the lowest-producing salesperson to take the same actions as the top salesperson, he or she would get the same results.

Clate asked, "How do I get him to do that?"

I said, "Every action we take—or do not take—is directly correlated with how we see the world. I can guarantee that your top salesperson sees Keap as a great place to work and loves the people, the company, and the compensation plan. The lowest-performing salesperson says, 'I hate this job. When are they going to improve the product? I am stuck at this place.'"

"So," said Clate, "what creates how we see the world?"

That brings us to our third principle.

Principle 3: Thinking, Speaking, Writing, and Doing

Our world is created by what we say to ourselves (our thoughts), what we say to others (our speaking), the things we write, and the things we do. Thinking, speaking, and writing are obvious; "the things we do" needs an explanation. If someone *says* that he can get anything done, but when an opportunity presents itself, he is afraid and doesn't try, then his doing trumps his speaking. Doing is language in action.

The document is one example of how both writing and speaking create our world. Every morning when I say my document, I say how much I love Amy and how much I appreciate her. I am creating my world through my speaking. Once when I was working with Karan Rai, he said, "Every time I'm here, you have your 'A' game on. How do you do it?"

I said, "It's not just me. You are creating your coaching experience by your speaking and thinking. You could undo the magic any time you wanted. When you woke up this morning in Manhattan and started getting ready for your flight, if you said, 'What in the world am I doing?' or when you got to the airport, if you said, 'Damn, this flight costs a lot of money,' you could undo it all."

That is why I am not casual with my speaking. It is creating my world. If someone calls me and says, "Call me when you want to chat," I will say, "I won't be doing that. I don't chat." Some people think I'm brusque, but creating my world through my speaking is more important to me than social grease. If I take my word casually, it takes away from my ability to create my future through my speaking. I am not willing to do that.

Chapter 25

Sacred Connections

H is cell phone rings. "This is Steve."

"Is this the Steve that coaches Ron and Mary Hulnick?" asks the caller.[3]

"One and the same."

"I want to talk to you about coaching—but I'm not sure I can work with you."

"Wait a minute. You just called me about coaching, then you said you aren't sure you could work with me. That's interesting. But let's start with *why* you couldn't work with me."

"You are a Mormon."

"And?"

"You believe in sin, redemption, hell—all that stuff. I'm an

---

[3] Ron and Mary Hulnick are the founders of the University of Santa Monica, which offered a Masters Degree in Spiritual Psychology.

atheist. I think all that is a little crazy."

"Let's get some things straight," says Steve. "There are certain things you would need to do if we worked together. First, I don't travel. You come to my office in Arizona. Second, you pay up front. Third, if you don't keep the agreements we make, your coaching agreement is finished. No refunds. Fourth, if you start believing in God or a religion while you are working with me, I will fire your ass. If you are an atheist, I want you to be a kick-ass atheist. I want people to be their best. I don't care what they believe. I care that they live what they believe."

Many of the people Steve works with are very spiritual. Some are also religious. Steve is both spiritual and religious, but when he steps into his office, he does not coach from his religion.

Steve works with people who believe in angels, auras, crystals, energy, shamans, Shakti, Jesus Christ, Moses, Krishna, and Allah, to name a few. He works with some people who access spirituality by attending church and some who do so by going on ayahuasca retreats. Some study the Torah. Some study *A Course in Miracles*. He honors each person for their belief and their spiritual processes. He works with each person inside their belief.

As a teenager, Steve had friends who were conservative Mormons and friends who were pot-smoking hippies—and everything in between. He has space for all kinds of people and all kinds of belief systems. His clients experience Steve's acceptance.

Melanie Waite says, "Steve is very nonjudgmental. Even though I'm a Mormon, if I were to say, 'I believe this part of Mormonism, but not that,' and 'I want to live this, but not that,' he would say, 'Okay, great. Let's make you the best non-Mormon Mormon there is.' He doesn't have a should or shouldn't."

Michael Serwa experiences Steve as Melanie does. He says:

Steve and I are so similar and yet so different. Here I am, a single man who doesn't want a committed relationship. I like to play the field with the ladies, and he got married at twenty-two. He's religious and I'm not religious at all. These are pretty big differences. But he has never had an element of judgment. He has never said, "Michael, when are you going to get serious and commit to one woman?" or "When are you going to find Jesus?" That would have put me off.

Many, like Michael, are pragmatic about the work Steve does. It is access to power in business, relationships, and life. Others find Steve's work deeply spiritual. They have had dreams, nudges, and divine confirmations about working with Steve. They hear the voice of God guiding them in their work. And then there are those who don't differentiate between the two. As Marianne Williamson writes, "The spiritual path is simply the journey of living our lives. Everyone is on a spiritual path. Most people just don't know it."

Perhaps the spiritual path is not just living our lives, but the journey of discovery while living our lives. Steve's work is a journey of peeling away the stories that keep you small, safe, and right. It is the journey of seeing yourself in all your humanity—fearful, insecure, and concerned about what others think. Yes, such a journey is disruptive. It is not for the faint of heart. But it is in this place of ultimate vulnerability that Steve helps you discover your magnificence—and you will never be the same. Whether that work is sacred or secular is up to you.

Chapter 26

The Cost of Coaching

"When I first learned about Steve Hardison," says coach Lisa Hale, "the first thing I heard, to be really blunt, was how much he charges his clients. I was kind of gobsmacked by that. My first thought was 'What kind of a coach would you have to be to command those fees?'"

Then she heard Steve has an extensive waiting list. It would take years if he were to coach everyone on the list. Twice gobsmacked, she considered, "What kind of a coach would you have to be to command those fees *and* have a waiting list that long?"

Steve answers that question with an analogy that is timeless, but which is spoken in the context of the early 2000s, when he first created it. He says:

If you go over to Bank One Ballpark at game time, you will see a man who is almost seven feet tall. His name is Randy

Johnson. He has won the Cy Young award five times. In 2004, he pitched a perfect game. That means you don't walk anyone. There are no errors. No one scores. There have been only twenty-three perfect games ever pitched in the history of Major League Baseball. Randy Johnson pitched a perfect game when he was forty years old, the oldest pitcher in the history of Major League Baseball to do so.

If you drive around the valley, you will see intersections where there are day laborers standing at the corners, hoping they will get hired that day for minimum wage. If you keep driving, you can find plenty of doctors and attorneys who are making six-figure incomes. If you drive to Bank One Ballpark, you can watch Randy Johnson pitch for the Diamondbacks. He is getting paid $52.4 million. Why? Because there are very, very few people who can pitch a perfect game and throw a baseball one hundred miles an hour. But that's not all.

If a pitcher throws the ball at one hundred miles an hour and it's right across the center of the plate, any Major League Baseball player can hit it out of the park. What makes Randy Johnson so valuable is he can throw a ball at one hundred miles an hour and he can put it on the edges of the strike zone so that when the batter connects, the ball will likely be on the ground or popped up.

The fewer people that can do something, the more a person who can do that thing gets paid. No one does what I do when I coach.

Scott Parker says, "Believe me, Steve is worth every dollar. When I was sitting with Steve, I never thought about the money. In fact, if anything, I thought he doesn't charge enough. I was thinking, 'This stuff he is doing is magic. This is the most unbelievable thing

I've ever seen.'"

But that's not the only reason Steve charges what he does. It is also about commitment. Lisa Haisha says, "Anyone who pays that kind of money is not going to pay it and then go back to who they were. Working with Steve is a really strong investment in your life. I'm going to get back tenfold of what I spent because it's going to shift who I am as a person. And that's what started happening. Just boom. Everyone was like, 'What is going on here?'"

There is yet another reason. "He charges that fee because of what it draws out of his clients," says Rich Litvin. "They have to tap into resources they never knew they had. They have to enroll their wife, husband, or business partner. And they have to show up in a way that never seemed possible before they chose to work with Steve. The value they get *before* they have even begun coaching with Steve is extraordinary."

Martine Cannon was so committed to work with Steve, that she was willing to sell her home. "I knew my life was more important than my property. But as soon as I was committed to selling my house, other options popped up. Someone said to me, 'You have plenty of equity in your house. Let's just release that.' I replied, 'I know that money can be released for renovations. Well, this [pointing to herself] is the house that is being renovated."

Jeff Dinsdale was twenty-three when he hired Steve as a coach. "I went through a lot to create the funds to work with Steve. My first day sitting in his office, I said, 'Now I know why you charge what you charge.'"

"Why is that?" said Steve.

"It is because now I know I don't need you."

"You got it."

If Steve is going to charge what he does, he had better deliver. Right? Nope. Steve is crystal clear on this. Ask him, and you will feel his energy start to rise. He guarantees that he will step into his office with one hundred percent of his heart, mind, and energy. The rest is up to his client.

"If you hire me thinking I am going to make it happen, you're nuts!" says Steve. It's a clear message he sends to each of his clients. "Clate, this isn't about me. It's about you," Steve explained to Keap's CEO. "Think of it as going to the gym and I'm your trainer. If I do the sit-ups, it's not going to make your abs tighter. This is on you. You are responsible to take what we create in the office and make it happen." It's a lesson that is sometimes learned the hard way.

Tom McGovern says of his coaching experience, "Frankly, one of my objectives wasn't met. It was a business goal. And clearly, it was on me.

"I recently looked back over my notes. The first note I read was something that I still haven't nailed down. Had I really embraced it, it would have changed the last ten years. Steve absolutely saw it and he had the solution for it. The stuff he shared with me and how he shared it was brilliant."

Steve recognizes that issues about money can be hard, but his focus is not on the cost. It is on the value. Stephen McGhee says, "The value he provides is exponentially greater than his fee."

Cost is quantifiable. Value is less so, but just as real. Aaron Benes says, "Every single session, there's at least one miracle, and usually multiple miracles. He got me to see my self-worth. I don't know how I could ever put a price on that."

Ethan Okura uses an analogy. "Without a doubt, the value I have received from working with Steve far exceeds the value I received from my Columbia Law School education, which I prize dearly."

One afternoon, Steve was coaching Andrew Leto. Andrew looked over at him and said, "Can I tell you something? You have earned your annual fee, just in what you taught me right now." That happened six times in that one session.

After the sixth time, Steve said, "You know, you have gotten $1,200,000 of value just from today. I'm a bargain."

Chapter 27

The Millennials

S teve doesn't coach for money. He charges what he does so people are committed and to grow his clients. Steve is clear there are things far more important than money.

Mark Silverman was ready to hire Steve, until he learned he would need to fly from his home in Virginia to Phoenix every two weeks. With two young kids, he knew "that ain't happening." But he stayed in contact with Steve over the next five or six years.

Mark was excited when he heard that Steve was speaking at Steve Chandler's and Rich Litvin's event in London. Here was a way to see Hardison face-to-face. Then Mark learned that his son had the opportunity to play baseball in Spain. Ten days of baseball and sightseeing in Spain—and Mark could go with him. It was at the same time as the London event. Mark called Steve and said he could fly from Spain to attend the event in London and then rejoin his son a day or two later. Steve said, "If you leave your son to come see me, I will refuse to see you. You spend every moment of those ten days with your son."

Other evidence that Steve's fees are a means to an end and not the end in itself are the people Steve has coached *pro bono,* particularly, those of the rising generation. Below, four millennials share their experiences with Steve in their own words.

Robert Harding

I was about seventeen years old. I was in high school. I was playing on the football team and enjoying life. We had what was historically a really, really horrible football team. Surprisingly, this year we put together a squad that was doing amazing and was making news, at least locally.

Steve came to one of our games. We were supposed to steamroll this team, and we were getting beat up in the first half. Steve came down to our sidelines. I didn't know who Steve was. To me, he was just some random guy running down our sidelines screaming at our players. At half time, he was in our locker room.[4]

I don't remember the full details of what he said. I just remember it really moved me. Steve was banging on lockers and telling us about our potential, how great we were, and how fantastic it would be for the city if we played well. He closed with, "You guys have the potential to be the greatest. Why don't you go do that?" We went out and played the best half of football our team had ever played.

A few months later, he was at our football banquet at the end of the year. Once again, Steve saw the potential in this group of high school guys. The school wasn't the most affluent. There were a lot

---

[4] Steve was there at the invitation of his friend and Mesa High's football coach, Kelley Moore.

of kids that needed help, kids who probably weren't going to go to college. He saw that.

At the banquet, he gave another awesome speech. Once again, I don't remember what he said word for word or even any of the highlights of it, but I knew in my heart that this guy knew what he was talking about. This was someone I needed to pay attention to. At the end of his speech, he made an invitation. "I have a dozen books here. Anybody is welcome to take one. Read it. I have my card in there too. If you had a good experience, give me a call."

I was eighteen. I had just gotten out of high school. I didn't want something to read. I wanted to have fun and do my thing before I went to college. But he had had such an impact on me, I picked up a book. Out of eighty kids, I was the only person who took a book. I read it in the next two days. I sent him an email and said, "Hey, this is awesome. The book was great. You've had such a great impact on me. I don't know what it means. I just feel inspired by you. I just wanted to let you know that."

I was the only person who reached out to him. I'm glad that I did because from there, he took me under his wing. I was a kid graduating from high school. I didn't have any money, but I met with him once a month, emailed with him, and called him. I took a lot of his time. Looking back, knowing how much people pay to be coached by him, it's amazing that he took so much time out of his busy schedule to coach an eighteen-year-old kid that had no prospects. I didn't know what I was doing with my life. He took time to share with me what was good in his life and what could be good in my life. A lot of things came from that one decision to reach out to him.

Every single second I was with him, his focus was one hundred percent on me. I felt like I was the only one in the world, even though his wife was in the other room, even though he had a million other things going on, even though I wasn't paying him a dime. I was his focus. That completely changed me. It helped me realize that his way of being was something I wanted to implement in my life.

I ended up converting to The Church of Jesus Christ of Latter-day Saints and going on a mission. Before I left on my mission, Steve committed me to make it the best experience I had ever had. He wrote me consistently. He helped me out financially. He was always, always there for me. He taught me to go out and create each day. Every day is a masterpiece. Go out and give it one hundred percent and create. That was always in the back of my head. As a result, I had a very successful mission.

When I came back home and started my own life, he was in the background of everything that I was doing. I didn't know he was talking me up to so many different people. I had no clue. I probably had a dozen job interviews because of him. I met his sons, Blake and Clint. I am partners with them in commercial real estate. I now have a career I can succeed with. Steve has set me up financially for the rest of my life. I wouldn't have this if it weren't for Steve. My best friends are his two sons. We have spent pretty much every day together for the past six years.

If I went back and stacked up all the hours that he spent on me, coaching me or putting me in a position to succeed, it would be hundreds of hours, simply because he wanted to help one kid out. Steve has altered the course of my life. And not just me, but now my son, and eventually my son's son. Generations to come have been completely changed.

Todd Runyan

I was a young teenager when I first met Steve. My family had moved in just down the street from him. We were in the same church congregation. A lot of people thought Steve was a little eccentric. Steve essentially doesn't care what anyone thinks about him.

I had my most profound experience with him when I was a junior in high school. I don't know how it happened, but I think Steve extended an invitation to meet with me to my parents. My parents and I met with him. It was an interesting meeting. Steve took Post-it notes and started sticking them on his head and going through some distinctions about thoughts and language. I remember I didn't really want to open up with my parents there. Steve picked up on that and asked me if I wanted to meet with him one-on-one. I took him up on that.

The biggest thing in my life at the time was sports. I was naturally really good at the 300-meter hurdles. Because the hurdles were spaced out, my hurdle form didn't need to be that good. I could catch up sprinting between the hurdles. So, I was pretty good at that event.

But the 110-high hurdles were a different story. That was a nightmare. I couldn't even run the race correctly in my head. Even in my visualization I was crashing.

Steve helped change all of that. I met with Steve for about a month, for four sessions. One of the things that came out of that was the creation of what Steve termed the "velvet bullet." He said, "I want you to feel like you're smooth and super fast over the hurdles."

That was cool, and it helped with my hurdles, but that wasn't the distinction that shifted things for me. It was when Steve said, "You are extraordinary, brilliant, and free." That one took hold of me and is still a part of me today. EBF. That enabled me to get out of my head.

I went from being a Junior Varsity athlete in that event in my sophomore year to fifth in the state in my junior year. And then in my senior year, I was the state champion. I attribute almost all of that to the work I did with Steve.

I have tried to do with other people what Steve did with me. I couldn't. It's not formulaic. You can't reproduce it by going through the steps. The best way I could describe it was that Steve was a conduit allowing me to see my potential. It's hard for me to overstate what he has done for me in my life.

Sebastian Hidalgo

I have known Steve since I was three years old. When my family moved into the neighborhood, Steve and Amy immediately came to our front porch with a warm welcome, a set of plastic drinking cups, and a trampoline for my siblings and me, who were all under the age of seven. My family's relationship with Steve quickly became intimate.

In 2012, when I was fourteen years old, Steve approached me, with his gleaming eyes, large smile and towering stature, and asked me if I would consider being his personal landscaper at his home. He told me that he would give me time to think about it and that we could arrange a date and a time for us to meet at his home and go over the responsibilities that I would be accepting. I accepted the opportunity.

We met on the given day, and he explained with great detail what he expected of me. At the time, my high school did not hold classes on Fridays, so I agreed to go to Steve's house each Friday morning to do my job. There were days when I needed to arrive as early as 3:00 and 4:00 a.m. in order to complete my work at Steve's and also fulfill other responsibilities for that particular day.

After each workday, I would let Steve know that I was finished for the day. We would then do a thorough walk-around of the exterior of his home to ensure that I did an acceptable job. He would praise me for my work, and then he would share invaluable life principles. Five of the principles Steve shared with me are:

1. **Limitation creates value.** If there were a million people who could play basketball like Lebron James, nobody would know who Lebron James is. The more limited you are, the more valuable you become.

2. **Whatever it is that you are doing in the moment, be the best in the world at it.**

3. **Create a lens through which you see the world.** You control what affects YOUR world. What you allow to enter your world shapes who you become.

4. **Be My Word (BMW). If you make commitments, keep them**. If Steve tells you that he will be at a certain place at a certain time, he will be there at that time. If he says he will spend X minutes with you, expect for him to spend exactly X minutes—no more, no less.

5. **Fear does not exist in the world.** I could never bring Steve a cup of fear. You cannot find fear. You can only create it in yourself.

Fast forward eight years. I had graduated from high school, served a mission, enrolled in college, and gotten married. Steve came up to me at church and said, "I'd like to give you this watch." It was a $3,000 watch. He had bought it in Switzerland. I loved it because Steve gave it to me.

A few months later, Steve asked me how my wife and I were doing. I said, "We're young and we're poor, just like any young married couple, but we are loving it." Steve offered to buy the watch back from me for what he originally paid for it. I refused. The gift has a lot more value to me than the $3,000 because it came from Steve. I was moved that he was essentially going to buy his watch twice so he could help us out. You're always going to win when you work with Steve.

David Bennett

I was a bad student in high school. We had an academically strong school, so bad around here is being a "B" student. That's about what I was. I was not really interested in college or med school. I was into building guitars. I'm good with my hands. I was going to do that for my profession. Then I realized that building guitars probably wasn't the best career choice. "Well," I thought, "I guess I'll be an orthopedic surgeon."

That isn't as random as it sounds. My little brother had arthrogryposis, which is a really severe bone defect disease. He had a bunch of surgeries at the Shriners Hospital in Utah. They actually lengthened his bones. So, orthopedics had caught my interest.

Steve was very encouraging. He thought it would be a great career and a great direction for my life. I said, "Yeah, but I'm not smart. How am I going to do that?"

Steve taught me that if I wanted something, I should write it ten times every day. He also taught me how to visualize my goal.

"All right. That's a simple thing." So, I started doing that.

I knew you had to get good grades to get into med school, but I had no clue how to do that. I used the visualization technique Steve taught me. Every single day I wrote it down: "I, David, get perfect grades."

I got great grades in undergrad and went to med school at Howard University in Washington, D.C. Steve and Amy flew out to my graduation. It was just my family and Steve and Amy. I did well in med school and matched into my first choice in orthopedics at the University of Arizona.

In all the time I spent with Steve, he never told me what I should do. I chose what I wanted to do, and he showed me how to reach it.

Visualizing has made me a better surgeon. Before every surgery, I go through every step in my mind. I usually write it out so my team also knows each step. I have found that the outcomes are far superior when I do that. It's staggering how much better the outcomes are. The surgery goes twice as fast, with about an eighth of the negative outcome. I learned that from Steve.

Of all the principles Steve taught me, visualization was the biggest one. I would say that is something everyone should know how to do. Honestly, I can't even imagine what my life would be like without it. Steve really helped me shape the direction of my life.

Chapter 28

TBOLITNFL

TBOLITNFL is a mouthful, until you realize it is simply the acronym for "The Best Offensive Lineman in the NFL."

But it is more than an acronym. It is a story, an event, a video, a website, and an experience. It appears to be about a football player. It's not. Lorraine Warren got that. Ten years after watching the video, she emailed Steve: "I remember you asking me to watch the video TBOLITNFL. What you don't know is that I cried for several days after watching that film. The possibility that I saw for my life really scared me and brought me to my knees."

TBOLITNFL provokes knee-buckling possibility. It is a wake-up call, but not like xylophone tones, birds chirping, or even annoying techno beeps. It's like the errant fire alarm in the middle of the night that jolts you out of sleep and shoots adrenaline through your system. It says, "Wake up. It's time to live big."

It was Sunday morning, September 5, 2010. Printed newspapers were still a thing. Steve was perusing the Arizona Republic and saw that Matt Leinart—a former starting quarterback for USC, a Heisman Trophy winner, and a first-round draft pick—had been released from the Arizona Cardinals. This man had talent, yet ESPN was saying nobody wanted to pick him up. The Arizona paper was saying, "He's a washout." Steve knew he could help Matt Leinart with the critical missing piece—his thinking—if he could speak to him in person.

Steve contacted his friend and former Arizona Cardinal, Vai Sikahema, who gave Steve the phone number for Deuce Lutui, a teammate of Leinart's. When Steve and Deuce connected on Monday morning, Steve explained that he could help Matt. "Deuce, it's what I do for a living. I work with people's thoughts. But I can't do it on the phone."

"So," said Deuce, "you only do this face-to-face?"

"Yes."

"You won't be able to help Matt then. He's gone to Texas. He's with the Houston Texans." That information had not yet been released.

Steve thanked Deuce and was ready to hang up when Deuce blurted out, "Would you do with me what you were going to do with Matt?"

Steve heard the hunger. He liked that. "Deuce, I can't do with you what I was going to do with Matt Leinart. You're not Matt. But I can do with you what I can do with you."

Deuce had one day off a week, Tuesdays. Steve invited Deuce to look at his schedule and find a Tuesday in the future where he could meet with Steve for two or three hours. Steve would make it work with his schedule.

"Tomorrow is Tuesday," said Deuce.

"I have clients tomorrow."

"Can I come tonight?" asked Deuce.

Steve could work with that kind of desire. Steve had a family dinner that night, but he agreed to meet with Deuce between his clients the next day. "And Deuce," said Steve, "come on time— American time, not Tongan time. If you're late, we don't meet."

Deuce showed up early. When Steve opened the door, a massive Tongan loomed in the doorway. Deuce was 6'4", 386 pounds. He filled up his 5X jersey. He had tattoo sleeves on his arms and legs. He looked formidable—except for his smile.

Steve invited him into his family room. "Deuce, tell me about yourself," prompted Steve. Deuce spoke about living in Tonga, coming to America, and the car accident that killed his sister and put his father and brother in a coma. He talked about his wife, his children, and his God. After forty-five minutes, Steve invited Deuce into his office.

Deuce took one step into his office and backed out. "What do you do in here?"

"We create miracles," said Steve.

Deuce took his sandals off and stepped in with reverence.

"Deuce, do you have anything else you want to say before we begin?"

Deuce spoke for forty-five more minutes. When he had nothing left to say, Steve said, "Deuce, I have just one question for you." Steve leaned forward in his chair. "Who is the best offensive lineman in the NFL?"

Deuce looked up in thought. He was checking his NFL Rolodex.

"Thanks for answering my question, Deuce."

"But . . . I didn't answer your question."

"Oh, you did. It was loud and clear."

"I'm confused. What are you talking about?"

"Okay. Let's change places. Just pretend I am Deuce Lutui. Ask me, 'Who is the best offensive lineman in the NFL?'"

"Okay . . . Who is the best offensive lineman in the NFL?"

Steve vaulted from his chair, grabbed Deuce by the shirt with both hands and roared, "IF YOU HAD ANY IDEA WHO I WAS, YOU WOULDN'T ASK ME SUCH A STUPID QUESTION!" Steve kicked his chair with his exploding energy. Then Steve brought the volume down and the intensity up. It was far more unnerving. "Listen. I am Deuce Lutui and *I am* the best offensive lineman in the NFL. That's who I am."

Steve stood up, smiled, and said in a conversational tone, "Deuce, we're out of time. I have a client coming shortly."

Deuce looked dazed. He stepped outside the office and slid into his sandals.

"Deuce," said Steve, "if you got that inside of you, your whole world would change."

Steve walked Deuce out to his truck. With each step, possibility dawned. By the time Deuce reached his truck, he said, "Steve, I want you to fly to St. Louis on Sunday. I want you to watch me play football. I want you to go to all my away games. I want you to come to all the home games. We can put you up with the team."

"Deuce, you can count on me *not* doing that. But I will make you one deal. Drive somewhere, sit quietly, and think about what happened in the past three hours. Then go to my website and read it carefully. Sauté in it. Read everything my clients say about working with me, but read it as if it were about you. If you do that, I will come to your first home game. If you don't want to do that, it was nice meeting you."

Clate Mask, Steve's next client, arrived as Deuce was climbing into his truck.

"Who was that?" Clate asked, as Deuce drove away.

Steve gave him the short version.

Clate said, "Let me know if you hear back from him."

That night at 9:50, Deuce sent Steve this email:

> A few things I wrote down after our session and going onto your website:
> This has locked my future and has secured my goals
> The best in the game!!!
> The best OL in the NFL!!! best pro bowler there is!!!!
> Best at my craft!!!! Best on the team!!!!
> Captain!!!!! PAID!!!!!!!!! I AM!!!!!!!!!!!
> The scary thing is this isn't enough for me nor good enough.
> Love you brother.
> I want you to witness this at every game, at every play. Please let me have you at every game you are able to make. It will bless my life to know you're behind me, literally watching my every move!
> Again, The best in the game!!! The best OL in the NFL!!! best pro bowler there is!!!! Best at my craft!!!! Best on the team!!!!
> Captain!!!!! PAID!!!!!!!!! I AM!!!!!!!!!!!
> Ofa atu,
> TBOLITNFL
>
> Deuce Lutui

At 9:50 p.m., September 7, 2010, TBOLITNFL was born.

The first thing Steve did was respond to Deuce: "Deuce,

powerful, like you. So let it be written. So let it be done!!!"

The second thing Steve did was give Clate an update. Clate wrote back: "I am a God-serving man, a great father, and the CEO of a billion-dollar software company called Infusionsoft." TBOLITNFL was only minutes old and it was already creating possibility.

Launching the Vision

True to form, Steve shared the Deuce Lutui story with his family, friends, clients, and the people he saw at the car wash, the mall, and the grocery store—pretty much everyone. Steve's son, Blake, told the owner of his company, who called Steve and asked him to come and share the experience with his company. Steve said, "That's not what I do." But the owner persisted. He touched Steve at a tender spot. "Your son works here. Come help our company."

Steve agreed. "I'll give you one hour."

They met at King's Fish House restaurant in Tempe. They expected twelve people. There were sixty. They were packed into a room that accommodated forty-eight. Steve shared the story with his signature passion. People were inspired, but not because one football player was electrified by his possibility. Deuce was the prototypical Everyman. People walked out of King's Fish House inspired by who they could be and what they could do.

The King's Fish House audience left inspired and in action. One person created a website where the written story was posted. One man rented a billboard so that for eight seconds out of every minute, twenty-four hours a day, for thirty days, "TBOLITNFL" flashed at the cars driving on the freeway.

Steve shared the story over and over, so often the tellings strained his voice. After Steve rasped the story to Dr. Gibson in

California, the doctor enrolled his friend, Julie Blake, a vocal coach, to help. Soon, she was on the phone telling Steve what he needed to do to restore his voice. When he could speak, Steve shared the Deuce Lutui story with her.

"Would you come to Utah and do what you did at the restaurant?"

"That's not what I do. And I don't love traveling."

However, it happened that Amy was presenting a paper at the Sperry Symposium at Brigham Young University on October 29, 2010. They were already going to be in Utah. If Julie wanted to make something happen on October 30, Steve would do it. Julie took on producing the event. She even got Steve to agree to do something he never does. He let her tape the event.

Fifty-four days after TBOLITNFL was born, Steve was standing in a room at the University of Utah, speaking to an audience of six hundred people. He spoke from his heart as he related the series of events that brought Deuce to his home. He re-enacted the pivotal moment in his office, with Chris Dorris acting as proxy for Deuce. Even though Chris had been at King's Fish House, even though Chris knew it was a re-creation, when Steve grabbed his shirt and got in his face, Chris was rattled. "I was so proud that he chose me for that moment. That was pretty great, but at the same time I was scared shitless. I was afraid this could actually get out of hand." It didn't. But Chris's shirt, his favorite Greg Norman shirt, was a casualty to Steve's exuberance.

Steve finished telling the story of Deuce, then he drove home his message. "Listen. Commitment rocks the world. You want something to shift in your marriage? You want something to shift at work? You want something to shift at school? Get committed. When you are committed, the world lines up to support your commitment.

Commitment has gravitational power. Everything you need moves to the commitment."

Steve read a statement by W. H. Murray from *The Scottish Himalayan Expedition:* "Until one is committed, there is hesitancy, the chance to draw back, always ineffectiveness . . . The moment one definitely commits oneself, then providence moves too. A whole stream of events issues from the decision, raising in one's favor all manner of unforeseen incidents, meetings and material assistance, which no man could have dreamt would have come his way."

Steve finished, "I give you the same challenge I gave Deuce. Go find a quiet place. Ask yourself, 'What is it I want? What is it I could commit to?' And look inside. Be quiet long enough to see something."

The Response

The emails came from every state in the United States. They came from Paris, Luxembourg, and Germany. They came from Russia, Australia, and the Czech Republic. They all had the flavor of this one: "I don't know who Steve Hardison is. I don't know who Deuce Lutui is, but what I do know is that I'm going to be the best confectioner in all of Scotland" (Isla Morrison). Isla's email came with two pictures: TBOLITNFL spelled out with cupcakes and TBOLITNFL spelled out with seashells on a beach.

A CEO in London wrote, "Hi, Steve. You, sir, are magic in motion. That document belongs deep in the fleshy tables of every heart. I have gone through it three times, made notes, and carry a small black notebook that has my own version of TBOLITNFL in it. It would be surprising if everyone reading this document doesn't create their own personal internal commitment." (Steve later called "personal internal commitment" *declarations*, or, cumulatively, *the document.*)

Fred Beljaars from the Netherlands wrote, "My coach sent me a video of Steve doing TBOLITNFL. I watched the long version three times in a row. Awesome! I was in love." David Gerber wrote, "I've watched TBOLITNFL five times and it impacts me in new ways each time I watch it."

Eric Lofholm wrote: "Hi Steve, Gary Henson sent me the info on TBOLITNFL. I was so inspired by it I shared it at CEO Space today where I spoke to 300 people. I will share the story with several thousand people in the next year during my speeches and webinars. Warmly, Eric Lofholm, The World's Greatest Sales Trainer."

Jenn Walter wrote:

I had never heard of Steve Hardison. To be honest, I thought coaches were for weight loss and athletes. Parker Winder shared with me Deuce and TBOLITNFL. I am a Packers fan, so my first thought was, "Who is this other football team and why would I care?" But I trusted Parker.

Holy Buckets, Batman! I believe I may have watched that video twice. Who is this man? Who talks like this? Who does this for another person? I was hooked.

Steve has no idea of my journey, but he helped put a spark in my mind that started a fire in my heart that fueled my passion for transformation. I am the creator and master of my life!

Four years after viewing the video, Emma Holmes in England wrote to Steve:

Hi Steve,

I hope you and dear Amy are well! I am not sure if I have shared this with you, but around 2016, I created my commitment as TBOSDJTITW = The Best Online Scratch DJ Tutor in the World. Shortly after, a leading DJ software company contacted me to create some video tutorials for them and referred to me as exactly that. I love sharing the TBOLITNFL video with my clients, and all who take the time to absorb it are transformed. Grateful for you.

Shortly after Rosie Bernardo moved from Los Angeles to Miami, she watched the TBOLITNFL video on one of her breaks at the school where she worked. She says, "I can't even explain what went through me, but basically, I said, 'Holy shit. Somebody is as loving as I am.' I had felt embarrassed about the acts of kindness I did. I felt like maybe they were over the top. This video gave me permission to keep doing them."

It also inspired her to "stick with this coaching thing," which she was doing on the side. Rosie relates:

I started giving the Steve Hardison video to people. One of the people I gave it to was my cousin, before he was the mayor of Miami. After watching the video, he literally drove to my apartment and he gave me a $100 bill. He said, "Thanks, coach." He had written his personal internal commitment on a napkin. This was before he was mayor, but he was already on that trajectory.

I started a coaching group called The Power 10. It was an after-school coaching program at the adult school. I had enrolled ten young adults in it. There was a young guy from Miami in this group. I believe his name was Adid and that he was originally from somewhere in Africa. Sometimes I substituted for the teachers at the school, teaching their English classes. Adid had been in one of the classes I had substituted and he wouldn't do anything. When he came to

The Power 10 program, I said, "Adid, can you just watch this video?" He agreed and started watching it. Shortly after, he said, "Miss Bernardo, this is boring."

"Just take it home, and watch it at home," I pled.

So, he went home and watched it. Two days later, he was frantically searching for me at the school. When he found me, he said, "Oh my goodness. I watched the video and I started crying. I don't even know why, but I was sobbing. So, I watched it again. I think I watched it five times. And then I started writing my commitments. I don't know what was going on, but all these words started coming out of me."

"Wow. You know what?" I said. "I'm going to tell Steve about you." So, I sent Steve an email and I asked if he would sponsor Adid. It cost $100 for each kid to take this training with me. Steve agreed and even wrote an email back to Adid.

I continue to send that video to every person I know when I think they'll be open to watching it. I send it to every client before I work with them. It doesn't matter who it is, every single person experiences a transformation watching that video.

Postscript

Deuce Lutui caught the vision of what he could do. He was on fire. He had a killer season. But ultimately, his football career floundered because of his weight. Deuce decided to move from the Cardinals to the Bengals. Will Keiper writes:

His lucrative new contract was conditioned upon him passing the Bengals' physical exam. Among other things, the exam included stepping on a scale to check his weight. In another single, powerful moment, Deuce's world changed again. The scale declared he was carrying 381 pounds; he should have been thirty or forty pounds lighter.

The Bengals said, "No, thank you Deuce," and less than twenty-four hours after he left for the promised land of his new contract and team, Deuce was on a plane back to Phoenix . . .

Some estimated that he left more than six million dollars over two years on the Bengals' table. If this was the case, it represented about $200,000 per excess pound he carried onto that scale in the Bengals locker room.

The next day he signed a modest, one-year contract with the Cardinals.

Deuce's final year as a Cardinal was bleak. Things went downhill from there. Does this disappointing conclusion invalidate TBOLITNFL? Only if TBOLITNFL was about a football player. It's not. Every time Steve shared Deuce's story, it was always about waking someone up to their own possibility and inspiring him or her to commit to making it happen. Deuce woke up. He was inspired. But he failed to do what he needed to do to make it happen. As such, the doleful finish of his football career is not a footnote to TBOLITNFL. It is not something to be swept under the rug. It is truth told in relief.

A personal internal commitment is not a magic wand. It is a powerful commitment that brings dreams into reality by consistent, daily actions. Miracles happened. Dreams were actualized. Chris Dorris, who stood in for Deuce at the University of Utah, concludes, "I cannot believe—I definitely will *not* believe—that the value of these powerful stories is in any way lost by virtue of someone either choosing a different path or forgetting their power."

Conclusion

TBOLITNFL continues to be read and watched. It has been more than thirteen years since Steve spoke at King's Fish House and the University of Utah. Steve still gets emails like this:

> Thank you for sending TBOLITNFL to me. I'm inspired by Deuce's commitment. It does the same thing for me that it appears to have done to the others who have read it. It makes me want to be my best. It makes me want to play bigger in every area of my life, to man up and take the challenge of me. I will watch in great expectation, and cheer on number 76 this year, with a love I have for the greatness in human beings when they're being all they can be. Thank you for all you've done in my life to bring out the greatness of me.

Man up. Woman up. Play bigger. Love the greatness in humanity. Tap into your own greatness. That is what TBOLITNFL is all about.

Link to TBOLITNFL video:

https://www.youtube.com/watch?v=3n7Kvu-KrEg

Chapter 29

TBOLITNFL
According to Chris Dorris

In October 2010, Steve called me and said, "Chris, you know Julie Blake, right?"

"Of course," I said. "I just spoke with her yesterday. She invited me to go to Utah for her event. I told her I was at the Fish House in Tempe when you did the original TBOLITNFL."

What I thought but didn't say was: "No way am I going to Salt Lake City. I am not going to miss an Eagles game."

Steve interrupted me. "She's having a hard time pulling this event together. This is what I want you to do. First thing tomorrow morning, at 7:00 a.m., call her. Do NOT tell her that I told you to do this. That is imperative. Call her and ask her what she needs. And whatever she asks for, say yes. If she asks for fifteen Harley

Davidsons, you figure it out. If you do this, I promise you will experience miracles in your life both personally and professionally. Are you willing to do this, Boatness?" (Steve calls me "Boatness." I call him "Admiral.")

"Yeah. Because I love you."

"Pray to God she asks for something huge." Click.

I jumped in because I love, love, love this stuff. I really do feed off of it. Now, we got game. Still, I was scared shitless and uber-energized. I was scared and pumped.

So, the next day, I called Julie. "Hey Julie, it's CD. Is there anything you need to pull this together? Because I know it's a big deal and you are really working your ass off."

Julie said, "Chris, you're a godsend!"

"What can I do to help you?"

"Can you please be at the event? It would be so great to have you here," Julie said.

I host a big party at my house every Sunday during football season. My house is the place to be. I hate missing games. But I made a commitment to say yes to everything. I told her I would be there.

"Oh, that's great," Julie said. "And can you pay for the venue?"

"What?!"

I thought, "I just hired Steve Hardison. How much disposable cash do you think I have sitting around? I'm freakin' broke. I'm pumped about it, but I'm broke."

But I committed to say yes to everything. I told Julie I would pay for the venue.

She said, "You probably want to know how much it is."

I guess I should have, but it didn't matter. If it were five bucks, I didn't have it. And it was thousands.

I said, "Game on."

She said, "Thank you, CD. Can you wire that to me tonight?"

I'm the yes man.

She gave me the wire information. I'm thinking, "I have to get the money."

I plopped down on the top of my stairs and sat there and thought. It took me forty-five minutes to come up with a solution. I was excited about my idea, but in retrospect I realize I should have sat with it for another fifteen minutes. I would have come up with a much better solution. But who cares? I came up with one. And all that matters is that there was one, one I would never have even considered if I had not taken that leap.

I had just made an agreement with a new corporate client to pay me in advance for some work I was going to do for them. I called and told them about TBOLITNFL and what I was doing and asked if I could come pick up a check that day. They said, "Oh, we'd love to be a part of that." The takeaway for me is that if I ever need to create anything, I can do it like *that*. That's what TBOLITNFL is all about in the first place.

I was on my way back from picking up the money from my client. I was all amped up because I felt like a freakin' powerhouse. I couldn't wait to get home and wire the money to Julie. I was also thinking about getting my plane ticket, since I was now going to Utah for the event. At this time, I was also in the middle of creating my first ever audio program, a five-hour course called "Creating Your Dream." I called the production company and said, "Can I get 500 copies of disc one? Can I get them tomorrow? Because I'm leaving tomorrow." I gave the discs out at the event and that led to clients. Miracles were already starting to occur. And they are still occurring.

So, I was driving and thinking about all this stuff, and my girlfriend called. I started telling her how excited I was. She said, "Hold on. You just hired this guy. And you're paying for his venue?" She's going off. I'm like, "Sister, you are so getting in your way here. You are not bringing this vibe down." And that vibe has never come down.

I went to the event in Salt Lake. Steve brought me up on stage. People are still talking about that. People hired me from that. I'm still using it. I created an "All In" audio program, which has now become an online course, and is now a fundamental element of my corporate training. I teach that goals are for those who don't have the guts to make a decision. A goal is, "Oh, I hope I can pull this off." A decision is, "This has to get done, like now."

Steve was right when he said, "I promise you, I promise you, you will experience miracles in your life both personally and professionally."

This story has changed my life.

Part Three

Steve Hardison—the Man

Chapter 30

Love

"Have I told you I love you today?" Steve asks Amy. He will ask again in a few hours, and once or twice more throughout the day. Amy opens the refrigerator. A sticky note clings to the milk. It reads, "Amy, I love you. Thank you for being my wife. Steve." The date stamp in the upper right corner reads, "Now and forever." The toothpaste bears another note. This one says, "I love you today. SFH." And there are the frequent refrains: "What can I do for you today?" and "Let me tell you how amazing you are . . ." Amy gets it. She knows Steve loves her. It is the bedrock of her world.

It is also signature Steve. Steve does everything with intensity, including how he loves. People notice. They can't help it. He speaks of his love for Amy openly, boldly, effusively. And it smacks of possibility.

Yayati Desai says, "I adore the way he treats his wife, Amy, and the love he has for her. It's inspiring. If all husbands around the

207

world were like that, the world would be a different place. I aspire to be like him. Being a coach like him is my second priority; being a husband like him is my first."

Dr. Lorraine Warren writes, "I love the way he speaks of his wife, Amy. I love the way he loves her. I love how much he loves her. I love her because of how much he loves her. It's infectious. And, I have never met her in person! I have even had the thought, 'I would love to marry someone who loves me the way Steve loves and cherishes Amy Hardison.'"

Amy and Steve, 2013

Who wouldn't? It's the stuff of fairy tales.

So, what is the secret?

It is not that Steve and Amy never fight. It's not that they are naturally compatible. It's not that they are natural soulmates. Their children have often asked in disbelief, "How did you two ever get together?" Their magic formula is simple. They constantly create their love and their relationship.

"You create love by what you say and what you think," says Steve. "When people fall in love, they say, 'She is the most amazing person I've ever met' and 'He is wonderful. I can't wait to see him.' They get married and a few years later they say, 'All she does is complain' and 'He's so selfish.' You create falling in love. You create falling out of love."

Steve uses an object lesson to teach this to his clients. When a client says he wants more love in his relationship, Steve writes a check for a million dollars and hands it to him. "Just bring me one cup of love and that check is yours." Steve has never paid out, "because the only place love exists is in language." This is the cup of love distinction. It is true for all the intangibles: trust, happiness, faith, love, etc.

Steve elaborates, "You don't have to create physical objects by your speaking. I don't have to say, 'chair, chair, chair' to have the chair exist. It's here. I can touch it. I can sit on it. But love is different. States of being don't exist in physical reality. If you want love, you must speak it into reality, every day. If you stop speaking it, it will disappear."

Consistent, intentional creation. Is that all it takes?

There's more.

Several years ago, Steve was getting ready to run some errands. He always makes sure to say goodbye and give Amy a kiss before leaving. On this occasion, they enjoyed some light-hearted banter.

"You know," said Steve, "it is going to be pretty rough on the women out there when I'm walking around looking this good."

"Well, you just remember you belong to me."

Steve got serious. He looked in Amy's eyes. He said, "I would never forget that. You healed me. You are everything to me."

This interchange reflects their love and devotion. It also reflects the work they have done to get to a place of unity and peace.

Steve has a healthy respect for the challenges of love. He frequently says that relationships are the hardest work we will ever do. Steve's daughter, Lil, relates:

> I went through a divorce when I was thirty-four. I had four-year-old twins. It was devastating and the transition was rough, but eventually I told my dad, "I am really pleased with where I am. You have been so supportive. You are here for me. I'm happy. I have everything I need. I don't need a relationship."
>
> I thought he would say, "That's great. I'm so happy for you." Instead, he said, "That's great to hear, but you are playing it safe. Relationships are where the growth is."

Indeed, nothing stretches our souls, exposes our weaknesses, or makes the constant demands on us like marriage and relationships. But it is because of this, not in spite of this, that relationships yield so much growth, and so much joy.

Love Beyond the Center

Amy is the center of Steve's universe, but surrounding that center are concentric circles of love that include Steve's clients, friends, and people he has just met. "Love is, I am that" is part of

Steve's document. He says it. He lives it. It shows up wherever he goes.

In 2002, Steve spoke at the University of Santa Monica's graduation ceremony. When it was his turn to speak, Steve walked to the podium and looked out at the graduates. He stood in the presence of his love. He was unhurried. He held the room in his eyes.

After five minutes in clock-time and an eternity in speaker-time, he boomed into the microphone, "I LOVE YOU." Then he sat down.

"Chills went up and down my spine," recalls graduate Stephen McGhee, the 2002 student of the year. "He didn't *talk* about love, he demonstrated it. It was the most powerful non-speech speech I have ever heard."

Love in Action

"Steve sees opportunity and acts on that opportunity," says Ward Andrews. "I think that is the difference. We all see the opportunity and maybe we step back. Steve steps forward. And he'll do it day and night. I received a text from him last week at 3:00 in the morning. It said, 'loving you.' At 3:00 in the morning!"

When Steve is present to love, he doesn't just bask in its warmth. He texts. He calls. He visits. He acts. Deanna Chesley writes, "I love that he will stop by my house just for a hug and then race off in his Porsche."

Steve is masterful at microbursts of love, but often he invests more time and effort. When he goes to Utah, he drops by and visits teachers who taught him in elementary school, junior high, and high school. He thanks them for taking an interest in him and for teaching him life lessons. By his actions, he tells them their life and their career matter.

When Steve learned that his good friend, Rick Glauser, was

dying of cancer, he called Rick and told him he was going to take off work and they could do whatever Rick wanted. "Rick wanted to take a farewell tour," says Nan Glauser, Rick's wife. "Rick wanted to see friends they went to high school with, people he had worked with, and some family. So, Steve drove up to St. George, picked up Rick and they drove around Utah for two weeks so Rick could say goodbye. It meant so much to Rick that Steve did this. If there is a word to describe Steve, it is love—kind, real, authentic, meaningful love."

Steve has coached Clate Mask, the CEO of Infusionsoft (now Keap), for over a decade. On occasion, Steve stops by their headquarters. He doesn't just focus on Clate or the executive team. He visits with everybody. Tara LaRue Stradling says:

> When I met Steve, I was Clate's executive assistant. I got to visit with Steve here and there. We became friends on Facebook. I posted two things on Facebook that he reacted to. Once, I posted about loving flip flops and he brought me a really nice pair of brand-new flip flops. Another time, I posted a meme about chocolate being bigger than my head. He brought me five or six Hershey candy bars taped together so I could put them beside my head and show that I found a piece of chocolate that was literally bigger than my head. That was so unexpected and so funny.

Steve notices and acts, not occasionally or when it is on his to-do list. It is his way of being. Stephen McGee says:

> I said something about Jesus Christ in a session once. I mentioned that, in my opinion, Jesus wasn't floating around in white robes. I think he was in people's faces. A week later, this big, heavy statue of Jesus Christ showed up at my house.

He does stuff like that all the time. A lot of people have the thought. The difference is Steve takes the thought and goes to Amazon, finds the statue, has it shipped to his house first so he can sign it, write about it, write on it, and then repackage it and ship it to me. I see all that stuff. Damn. . . Damn.

Clients

Steve loves his clients. He gets weepy just thinking about them. They feel it. Michael Schantz says of his coaching sessions: "I experienced his absolute dedication to me and my path while I was with him. For those two hours, I was given his undivided attention, heartfelt listening, and unconditional support. In short, I was engulfed with love. That was my experience with every coaching session with Steve for about a year and a half."

Karan Rai says:

I tend to hold myself to pretty high standards, and I hold others to high standards also. So, it takes a lot to impress me. But Steve has impressed me time and time again. Of all the amazing things he does, it is his level of compassion that has impressed me more than anything else. One specific occasion stands out.

It was one of those times when I was feeling stressed out about something or other. We were having this conversation about what's important in life, and he looked at me and said, "What are you stressed about? You're going to die. And none of your problems are going to go with you."

Then he said that we were going to visit one of his former clients. He was a high-powered attorney. He had made a lot of money. He was in his seventies and was struggling with dementia. He was living in this home that was a care center.

We drove to the care center. Even though this was the first time I met this gentleman, I could see he was just a shell of his former self. I don't even know if he recognized Steve. The thing that will always stick with me is how Steve held his hand and caressed his hair. He was so present with him. It was so beautiful to watch a man be that present with another man. We spent about an hour with him.

There are so many things that Steve does that are absolutely incredible: his ability to get you to see the big picture, his ability to get you to believe in yourself, his ability to take really complex issues and make them so simple, his ability to get you to take action. But the thing that inspires me the most is the depth of his humanity and his compassion.

Stephen McGhee says, "Steve has taught me so much about openness and loving and really being a man—a strong, grounded man with heart, with ferocity and velocity, but also with true loving."

Strangers, a.k.a. Friends

"Steve loves people on sight," says Tara LaRue Stradling. "He is unlike anyone I have ever met." Indeed, Steve loves big, and he falls in love quickly. Stephen McGhee says, "I've seen it a number of times. A cab driver would come pick me up after a coaching session and before the cab driver would drive off, Steve would be hugging the cab driver. This is in five minutes."

Steve's son, Clint, makes this observation:

He's always meeting people. He's constantly having interactions with people, the frequency of which would be exhausting. He has this impactful interaction with the cashier at the grocery store and then with the guy at the gas station and then with the woman who owns the dry-cleaning business. That takes so much sheer energy, enthusiasm, and interest in other people. It also takes confidence. He is bold in ways that I would never be. And because he does that, he then finds himself up to his elbows in somebody else's problems, but he is willing to jump in and help them solve them.

One time he was at the Arizona Center in Phoenix and there was a woman selling popcorn from her popcorn machine. He watched her for a few minutes and then the next thing I know, he is coaching her on how to create more business. For him, the stakes are extraordinarily low. But he sees that for her, the stakes are extraordinarily high. He sees how she could be a more effective version of herself. As they speak, she says that she doesn't want to always be selling popcorn. One day she wants to be like Iyanla Vanzant. So, dad pulls out his phone, calls Iyanla and then hands his phone to the popcorn woman.

Steve loves this sort of thing. When he retires—if he retires—he envisions plenty of days where he meanders around, meeting people, and helping them. But he is not waiting until retirement.

LaTrina Williams was the manager of the CVS drug store close to where Steve lives. On the day after Thanksgiving in 2015, Steve walked into her store with a tangle of non-working Christmas tree lights in his hand. He said, "I need to replace these." LaTrina relates:

During that short interaction, a sense of peace came over me. I didn't want to seem weird, so I continued to focus on showing him the lights. Once we were at the register, Steve asked if we had been open on Thanksgiving and if I had been able to enjoy Thanksgiving dinner with my family. I explained that we were open on Thanksgiving and my family lives in Louisiana. After I said that, it was like "Stop the presses!"

Steve said, "So, you had to work on Thanksgiving, and you didn't have dinner with your family? Did you at least have a Thanksgiving dinner?" When I said no, Steve said, "I'm calling my wife Amy. You're going to come and have dinner with us." I was floored, overjoyed, and nervous.

When the day came, I was at peace all over again. I was welcomed by the Hardisons as if I were a family member coming home for a visit.

Since the first day Steve and his family came into my life, it hasn't been the same. Steve has given me books, encouraged me with kind words, and stopped by the store to give me hugs. He has been a father figure, a role model, a big brother, the favorite uncle, a man that I'm honored to say I know and love.

The love that Steve has for his wife, his family and friends is a delight. How can one person have this much love and express it to everyone? I am grateful to be a recipient of the love that Steve Hardison possesses.

Steven Pothier, the ecclesiastical leader of the Mormon congregation where Steve worships, recalls the Sunday when Steve was teaching a class for the men. "I remember Steve bringing in a man who was blind and who sold brooms on a corner near our homes to share his story. I had passed by him at least weekly. Steve Hardison gave me the chance to actually get to know this man. This is clearly something the Savior would have done. It is far more appropriate than just speaking about Jesus's teachings."

How did Steve get to know this man and his story? Steve was driving home when he saw a man standing on the corner in the 115° heat, selling brooms and mops. Steve pulled into the parking lot and started visiting with him. He learned his name was Sebastian Ibañez and he was from Mexico. He was here earning money to send to his family. Steve drove to Rosa's, the local Mexican food restaurant, and bought him a bottle of Mexican Coca-Cola. Whenever Steve drove by, if Sebastian was on the corner, Steve would take a few minutes to stop, visit, and buy a broom.

Over time, Sebastian told Steve about the adversity he had encountered in his life, including his blindness. He also attested that God had watched over him. Steve asked him if he would be willing to come and share his experiences with Steve's church class. He agreed. By the time Sebastian was finished, more than a few men had tears in their eyes, and by the end of the week, many had new brooms.

Conclusion

Michael Serwa says of the time he spent with Steve in Arizona:

My coaching experience with Steve was phenomenal. Even just walking into his house was amazing. Here is this compassionate, giving, Jesus-loving guy, with all these kids and all these grandkids, and what is the first thing I see? A big picture of himself on the wall. I love that.

Who says that you have to choose other people over yourself? Or that if you love yourself, it's somehow selfish? Steve is definitely not selfish, but he sure as hell loves himself, and I think that's apparent to anyone who interacts with him. It really goes well with a theory that I have: for us to be able to truly love other people, we have to truly love ourselves first.

Perhaps Michael is on to something. Yes, Steve truly loves himself. But perhaps he has also tapped into eternal love, the kind that is limitless. Perhaps that is why after Steve has loved himself, there is plenty of love left over, so Amy feels like the most-loved woman in the world. And enough left over so his clients experience "a tsunami of love" (A. J. Richards). And enough left over to care about the blind man on the corner and to befriend LaTrina at CVS. And enough left over to love the person he will meet tomorrow, and the next day, and the day after that.

Chapter 31

We'll Have Fun, Fun, Fun

Jeff Dinsdale is a close friend with Steve's son, Blake. He also hired Steve as a coach when he was twenty-two years old. In 2010, Jeff went with Steve, Blake, and Blake's wife Maryn to an auto show in Los Angeles. He relates:

> We were spending the night at Steve's buddy's house in Redlands, California. Blake and Maryn were sharing a room and Steve and I were sharing a room. Early the next morning, I woke up and looked over at Steve. He was getting dressed in this kaftan thing. By the time he was finished, he looked like a Middle Eastern prince. He had even painted his face a little bit. This was out of nowhere. There had been no discussion about this.
>
> I started laughing and said, "Where are you going, man?" He just said he was going out. When he finally came back, I asked him where he had gone. He had gone to McDonald's

for breakfast and then to LA Fitness. He had been walking around meeting people.

That stands out to me because I think a lot of people think of Steve only as this powerful, transformational guy. They don't see how fun Steve is. It's the fun that makes the magic. What is life if you're powerful and you have all this money and you can do all this stuff, but you don't enjoy life? Steve enjoys life at a level that I have never seen with anyone else.

Steve definitely enjoys life. He enjoys chortling with comedians. He has a penchant for practical jokes. Amy, his kids, and even his grandkids know that if they leave the dining table for a minute, they are going to have to look for their food when they return. They know who is responsible. Steve delights in being playful. He always has.

Steve, Burford, England, 2019

Steve's siblings have plenty of stories to share. Steve's sister, Jayme, recalls:

We were all together in Utah when my mother passed away in 1993. A couple of days after the funeral, we all went to a mall in Salt Lake. There were benches in the middle of the walkways that were set up back-to-back. We were on one side and some strangers were on the other side. There wasn't enough seating for all of us, so Steve got up and walked away and took Kresta, our niece, with him.

In a few minutes, they came back and he said to the people on the other side of the bench, "We are with mall maintenance. We need to move this bench. Could we ask you to get up?" So, of course, the people got up and walked off. Then he and Kresta moved the bench two inches and then we all sat down.

Amy was embarrassed. You would think she would have been used to his shenanigans by then. So, she got up and walked down the walkway, looking at store windows. Steve is calling after her, "Amy Hardison, you can't get away that easily." He kept on calling after her and she was like, "Who is this person?"

We always have a lot of fun when we are together.

The "mall security" gag is one Steve recycles. He loves to see what people will do when someone speaks with authority when asking them to do preposterous things.

One hot summer day, Steve and his family were floating down the Salt River. There are several starting points for tubing this river. All that is needed is a parking area and a bank with a gentle slope into the river. There are no park rangers around for miles. At the location Steve and Amy had chosen, a crowd of sixty or so people were wading into the water. Steve raised his voice and spoke in his most official tone, "Excuse me. We need to inspect your ice chests. Please line up over here." Almost everyone did. Some even got out of the river, went back on shore, and got in line to comply.

On another occasion, Steve and his family and some friends were attending an Easter pageant. Several temporary restrooms were set up. When Steve walked into the men's restroom, he decided to have some fun. He announced that they needed to move the restrooms over a few feet. Would everyone please hold on. The men complied, with sidelong glances of "What the heck?"

Steve's fun is spontaneous. When a joke pops into his mind, he goes with it. When Steve, Jeff, Blake, and Maryn were pulling up to Paul and Melanie Waite's house on their way to Los Angeles, Steve said, "Jeff, I am going to tell Melanie that you are deaf and mute. Just go with it."

"Done deal," said Jeff.

The friends greeted each other and started catching up on the latest. Jeff says, "Everyone is talking, except for me. Steve explains I'm a client, a friend of Blake's—and deaf and mute. Melanie is as sweet as it gets. She was so sympathetic."

After a while, they started to make dinner plans. "They wanted to go somewhere nice for dinner. Steve asked me through pantomime where I wanted to go. I pulled out this coupon I had in my pocket. It was for free fries at McDonald's. I started pointing to the word 'McDonalds.' You could tell Melanie didn't want to go to McDonalds, but she didn't want to go against me, this poor guy that couldn't hear and speak."

Steve's fun often has an impish quality. Shanti Zimmerman currently lives in Switzerland, but she is originally from Arizona. When she returned to Arizona for a visit, she posted that she was in

Phoenix. Steve responded and invited her to work out with him at CrossFit. She accepted.

During their workout, Shanti was doing handstands—not an easy feat. She says, "You have to fight for a handstand. Every time I was doing one, Steve would come over and kick it out from underneath me. He was being really, really, really cheeky. There is definitely a part of him that is mischievous and playful."

Fun on the Internet

"Social media is so often an outlet for self-indulgence and glorification," observes Adam Amin Mahboubi. "Everyone I know, including myself, plays into that. I think it's interesting that Steve posts things you would never expect to be posted, super random, super joyful things." John Vehr says more candidly, "You've seen Facebook posts from him, right? They are crazy. He posts shit that the rest of us would say, 'I need to edit that.'" Steve doesn't care. He is having fun.

One of the things that Steve loves to do is to create contests and post them on his Facebook page. He has sponsored a "Guess what is the last thing I do before I go to sleep" contest and a "Fill in the blank: Amy says I should have been a _____" contest. The first person to respond with the correct answer wins a prize. Sometimes it is a $500 gift card. Sometimes it is simply going to lunch with Steve, who rarely does business lunches.

Steve's favorite contests have been for concert tickets. Amy is not a hard rock fan, so when a group comes to town that Steve wants to see, he creates a contest. He asks people to tell him why he or she should be the one to go with him to the concert. He has done it twice. Once for Jethro Tull and once for the Rolling Stones. The answers are fascinating. Sometimes the answers are so good Steve buys additional tickets. With the Rolling Stones concert, Steve upped the ante. Steve embedded in his contest rules the requirement of mentioning the name of his turtle. If you were a regular follower of his Facebook posts, the answer was easy.

The winners of the Rolling Stones contest were Gary Mahler, Bryan Samuels, and Curtis Marsh. Gary is a client of Steve's. He flew in from Canada to attend the concert. Curtis and Bryan flew in from out of state. Curtis says of the evening, "We danced, sang, and laughed like it was the last concert we would ever be attending. Four guys, three of whom had never met until that night, and we created a memory that is forever tattooed on my heart. Sometimes one gets to catch lightning in a bottle."

In case you are wondering, the last thing Steve does each night is squirt on some cologne. And Amy thinks this master delegator missed his calling. He should have been a king.

Dancing like a Star

"While Steve is a human dynamo wherever he is," says Curtis Marsh, "that's most true where the music's loud, live, and rocking"—especially if the music just happens to be "Walk This Way" or "Play That Funky Music White Boy" or "All Right Now." When Steve hears those songs, it is a dance party, wherever he is. Jackie Skinner connected with Steve during his driving adventure to Salt Lake City. She relates:

I met Steve for lunch in downtown Salt Lake. He accidentally left a gift he had been given at our table. I didn't notice this until about fifteen minutes after he left. I texted him about the forgotten gift, and in about ten minutes, Steve showed up in his awesome white car (I don't know cars well, but it's a nice one!) with the music full blast. He pulled up to grab the gift, with the music blasting, and the two of us danced on the busy sidewalk. A window washer was right next to us, and he laughed and laughed. It was a solid minute-long dance party, and then he zoomed off.

Steve dances with abandon. He doesn't care if he is at a concert or on a busy city street or in Home Depot or at a mall—or anywhere else. When he feels the music, his energy surges and he starts to move. He merges with the music. Steve is in a zone of absolute self-expression and pure bliss.

Emma Holmes says, "Steve is pure light, love, kindness and generosity. He is also playful, fun and energized." He is enlightened and outrageous. He is intensely focused and gleefully cheeky. He is not either/or. He is both/and.

As Carla Rotering says, "His playfulness is intertwined with the rest of who he is, which is really delightful."

Steve in his Halloween costume, 2019

Chapter 32

Making Sense of Steve

The nuns in the abbey break out in a song that is so snappy it is hard not to sing along. It is the second scene in the classic movie, *The Sound of Music*, just after Maria twirls in an alpine meadow. The nuns are trying to make sense of Maria, their atypical novitiate. They differ in their opinions about Maria but agree that the task of understanding her is as challenging as catching a cloud, pinning a wave upon the sand, and holding a moonbeam in your hand.

The same could be said for Steve. He defies easy explanation. He does not fit in classic categories. He simply isn't standard. Jason Jaggard reflects:

> Steve goes to a pedicure place and has exclamation marks painted on his toenails. Who does that? That is not normal. He does these weird things. That's probably the headline for Steve Hardison: "Who does that?" And that's what makes him so wonderful. His way of being is a threat to normality.

He radically accepts normality and radically disrupts it at the same time. And that is a really fascinating experience.

The consensus is that there is no one quite like Steve. Here is a sampling from a friend, a family member, and a client. John Goodie says, "I've never met a person like him in my life. And I've met a lot of people." Steve's sister, Teresa, says, "Steve is not like a lot of people. There's not another Steve, not that I know of." Clate Mask says, "Steve is so different than anybody I've ever met. Everybody you meet is different, but he's more different than anybody."

Indeed, most people don't turn their son's wisdom teeth into pendants for a necklace, which they wear. Most people don't keep their kidney stones and use them for the center stone of a ring. Most people don't frame an MRI of their brain and hang it in their house. Most people don't frame a close up of an ant so they can tell people, "This is my favorite ant (aunt)." Most men don't wear patent leather, fuchsia Oxfords. But Steve is unique, pathologically unique. Is it any surprise he pronounces "unique" as "**you**-ni-Q"? He thrives on zigging when others zag. He delights in leaving people slightly befuddled.

John Vehr says it this way:

If you look at a bell curve, something like 80 percent of people are in the middle. And then 10 percent are on each side, the outliers. Steve doesn't fit on the bell curve. He doesn't even fit with the outliers. He is kind of broken, and I mean that in the most loving, kind, and honoring way I can say it. Because he is broken, he doesn't see the world the way the rest of us do.

No doubt, Steve is difficult to decipher, but that doesn't mean we aren't going to try.

Steve, 66 years old, 2021

Nature

Steve entered this world with genes from two powerhouses. "My mom," says Steve's sister, Teresa, "was intuitive and perceptive. She could figure out people really fast. She was very intelligent. Our father was intelligent and very creative. That is in Steve's DNA. Steve has always thought at a higher, more creative plane."

Steve's sister, Jayme, adds this insight:

Steve would have known our dad less than anybody, and Steve is the most like him as far as charm, personality, and making friends. My dad was tall and very good-looking. There are a lot of similarities. Steve is not like him in the bad aspects. In my dad's later years, he did a lot of things that nobody would be proud of. But Steve was never like that. Where my dad chose some self-destructive paths, Steve chose to make something of his life.

Steve only has a few memories of his father. The opportunities for direct modeling were limited. This suggests that when Steve exhibits his father's traits and behaviors, genetics is in play.

In 1995, Steve and Amy made a trip to Adairville, Kentucky, where Roy Hardison grew up over sixty years before. It was like stepping into Mayberry. It had an old-fashioned town center built around a square park with mature, shady trees. There was a colonial-style town hall in the town center, complete with a clock tower. There was a barbershop with a red, white, and blue barber pole and a wooden bench that invited folks to sit a spell and gab. Three elderly men sat on the bench. As Steve approached them to ask directions, one man raised his voice and said, "You must be Roy Hardison's son." It stopped Steve in his tracks.

"How did you know?"

"You walk just like him."

The power of genetics is amazing, and slightly creepy. In Steve's case, it accounts for his charm, his fastidiousness, his propensity for practical jokes, his ability to talk the birds out of the trees, and probably several other unrecognized connections to a father who was absent yet present, if only at a molecular level.

Nurture

Maurine Hardison had a bit of the rebel in her. For Pioneer Day, the holiday celebrating the pioneers' arrival in Utah, she shaved Steve's and Phil's hair into mohawks. It got them kicked out of grade school. It was just too edgy for 1962. Decades later, Amy remembers Maurine dropping one-liners here and there, encouraging her to question authority. It was a lost cause. Amy colors inside the lines. Maurine was more successful with Steve. He questions authority, organizations, rules, paradigms, and all status quo thinking. Maurine would be proud.

Maurine, about 1985

This was not the only attitude Maurine bequeathed to Steve. Maurine had moxie. She was a natural-born CEO. She radiated "Don't mess with me—or even think about it." No doubt there is a genetic component to the transmission of these assertive traits, but there was also plenty of modeling.

Maurine gave her children a lot of leeway to experience life, to fail, and to learn through natural consequences. Maybe this was by necessity. In a pre-cellphone era, Maurine simply couldn't be too hands-on as a mom when she was rarely at home.

Teresa notes, "In the early years, Steven wasn't constrained. My mother wasn't teaching him a lot of things. My dad wasn't there. As siblings, we were all doing our own thing. No one was putting restraints on Steve's creativity." No one was reining in his ideas. No one was demanding he adhere to social conventions. He was a free spirit with plenty of space.

Steve's son, Clint, observes:

> I have a unique dad. He's unique in a lot of ways. I have spent a lot of my life pondering, "Who is this guy? Why is he like this?" I think he came that way. I think that he is wired differently. I think the nature of his childhood added to it. He had to learn to survive and he had to be creative in ways other kids didn't have to. That cultivated skills in him that other people don't have to cultivate.

Amy certainly never had to get creative to make sure she ate. Neither did Steve's kids. When Steve was young, he bounded down the stairs in the morning hoping there would be thirty-five cents on the table for lunch money. It was hit and miss. But hunger is a great motivator. It kicked Steve's creativity into high gear. He came up with a lot of ways to get food, some of which were even legal.

So many of the exceptional talents and abilities that Steve has today can be traced back to his childhood experiences. But there was also a dark side. There was trauma. There was a sense of abandonment. There was literally living on the wrong side of the tracks and being the kid that parents didn't want their children hanging out with. There was not fitting into the establishment, be it church, school, or community. There was having too much energy, too many words, and too much unbounded zest—aka a penchant for trouble. Steve internalized all these things and adapted accordingly. Some of his adaptations were empowering. Some haunted him for years.

Louise Phipps Senft observes, "I think Steve was deeply

wounded as a child and has probably spent his whole life trying to overcome his woundedness. It is a lifetime journey. He will possibly never be fully healed until he moves over the veil into pure spirit. But he's wired as a fighter. His big fight kept him alive."

The Dichotomy

Steve is crazy about black and white. Just look at his toenails. He frequently sports black polish with white exclamation marks.

Steve (left), Phil (right), with mohawks, Matt Mason (center), 1963

Sixty percent of his clothing is black or white or both. His cars are black or white. Birthday and Christmas gifts are often black and white: black-and-white-striped shirts, black-and-white Oxfords and customized Vans—black with white exclamation marks.

Steve is awash in dichotomy. It extends to his personality. Deanna Chesley says, "Steve is one of the most reverent and irreverent people I know." Scott Law notes that Steve is both humble and confident at the same time.

Steve loves hard rock and pan flute music. He is an extreme extrovert and basks in his alone time. He is both edgy and conservative. He is extremely picky when it comes to the taste of meat and he delights in odd culinary combinations, like a sandwich

233

Steve, 2017

of peanut butter, jelly, cheese, pickles, and ham. He is a veritable noise machine, loud, talkative, and boisterous—and he is disrupted by loud noises. He is absolutely enlightened and transformed—and he has meltdowns that are anything but enlightened.

It is perplexing. He is perplexing. As Carla Rotering notes, "He's a rascal. He's a motorcycle guy. He's a Mormon. He's all of those incredible, conflicting polarities." And then some.

Energy and Intensity

Steve Chandler, who knows Steve as well as anyone outside of his immediate family, says, "His energy is simply higher than anyone's I have ever met. Sometimes it's overwhelming to people. Sometimes it's just too much, even though it's benign, even though

Steve, 1994

it's loving."

To get a sense of Steve's energy, picture Niagara Falls—colossal, commanding, dynamic. Steve's sister Teresa says, "Steve is not for a faint-hearted person because his energy will burn other people out." That's not hyperbole. He burned out companions on his mission. When in the midst of a project, like sharing TBOLITNFL with the world, he can put in twenty-hour days while his family lags in exhaustion. When he sees possibility, he is like a horse with blinders, running at top speed and barely aware of the horses dropping out of the race. On the upside, his energy produces unbelievable results.

In addition to Steve's boundless energy is his intensity. Steve is intense as a way of being, but at the same time his intensity is not always activated. Think of a sports car that goes zero to sixty in 1.9 seconds. Steve's intensity is always there in potential, ready to respond when he hits the gas. Amy explains, "He may be having a totally normal conversation on the phone and the next thing I know, he is yelling and gesticulating. When the phone call is over, he is totally calm and says, 'I just needed to wake someone up.' The passion erupts because he cares so much."

Like his extreme energy, his intensity can be difficult. Adam Amin Mahboubi says, "I would say one of my most challenging things with Steve has been his intensity. He is by far the most intense person I know. And that comes across in his emails, his phone calls, and his Facebook posts. But once you accept that this is actually who this guy is and that he's not messing around, that's really amazing."

Steve's intensity means that every characteristic he has, every trait he embodies is supercharged. He is not just emotionally sensitive. He is *extremely* emotionally sensitive. He is not just high energy. He has more energy than most people have ever seen. He is not just amazing. "He is a walking miracle" (Steven Sainato).

A Highly Sensitive Person

When asked what makes Steve Steve, the people who know him best—his siblings, Amy, his children—all mention, "He came like that." But what is the "that"? Could that "that" hold the secret of Steve?

Fifteen to twenty percent of people are born with a neurological system that is prewired to be highly sensitive. They are considered "highly sensitive persons" (HSP), a term coined by Elaine Aron, a clinical research psychologist and pioneer in the field of high sensitivity.[5] High sensitivity exists on a continuum. Some HSPs consider themselves extremely sensitive, others quite a bit sensitive, and still others just moderately so. Steve never does things part way. He definitely falls into the extremely sensitive category. Many, but not all, HSPs are quiet and reserved. Thirty percent are extroverts. An extremely sensitive, extroverted HSP, like Steve, would fall into a narrow category of people who might be born "like that."

HSPs have strong reactions to things. While most people tune out sirens, glaring lights, strange odors, clutter and chaos, HSPs are disturbed by them. They may even find them physically painful.

HSPs are more aware of others' emotions and are intensely affected by them. HSPs will notice small sounds, tiny distractions, smells, or tastes that others aren't even aware of. Aron explains, "Most people walk into a room and perhaps notice the furniture, the people—and that's about it. HSPs are instantly aware, whether they wish to be or not, of the mood, the friendships, the amenities, the freshness or staleness of the air, [and] the personality of the one who arranged the flowers."

Highly sensitive people are often very intelligent, creative, exceptionally intuitive, compassionate, and spiritual. Their oversensitivities enrich and amplify their talents, so much so that they veer into the domain of giftedness. On the flip side, because they take in so much sensory information, they are more easily overwhelmed and stressed out than non-HSPs. When the onslaught of sights, sounds, and emotions becomes too much, they may get upset, frazzled, and angry.

---

[5] For more information on HSPs, see Elaine Aron's groundbreaking book, *The Highly Sensitive Person* (1996).

Not Your Average Joe

Many HSPs feel like they don't fit in. They fear they are out of step with the rest of humanity, even broken. Mel Collins writes, "For the first three decades of my life, I was convinced that there was something wrong with me. I seemed to feel things more deeply than those around me and processed my emotions for longer . . . As a child, I heard consistent messages of 'stop being so sensitive,' but I didn't know how to stop something that was naturally a part of me."

Studies have shown that HSPs don't just behave differently; their brains actually work differently than the brains of non-HSPs. Jerome Kagan of Harvard concludes that HSPs "are a special breed. They are genetically quite different, although still utterly human, just as bloodhounds and border collies are quite different, although both are still definitely dogs."

Little wonder non-HSPs are left scratching their heads when they are with an HSP. No surprise that most of us don't know quite how to explain Steve. John Patrick Morgan says:

> There are very few people I meet that I can't understand where they're coming from or what their reality is, especially after spending some time with them. Usually, I can anticipate what they will say. But Steve's responses continuously come out of left field. I definitely can't anticipate them. It's like he blindsides me every time, in a good way. My interest in working with Steve is to be able to see the world that he sees.

Awareness and Intuition

One of the central traits of HSPs is that they pick up on the subtleties around them. Be it sights, sounds, or emotions, they are aware of things that a non-HSP would never see. When Steve and Amy pick up a rental car or accept delivery on a piece of furniture or do a walk-through with a contractor, it is Steve's job to inspect. He sees everything, from the smallest scratch to the tiniest variance in alignment. It is a remarkable ability—and it can be frustrating. It sets a high bar for contractors. Steve can be seen as picky. When younger, the relentless awareness of a flawed world was a constant, low-grade irritation.

This hyperawareness is why HSPs are highly intuitive. An HSP processes sensory information both consciously and subconsciously, whether they want to or not. It is the subconscious processing that leads HSPs to say they "just know things" without knowing how they know them. In fact, Aron defines intuition as "picking up and working through information in a semiconscious or unconscious way." Aron elaborates, "You 'just know' how things got to be the way they are or how they are going to turn out. This is that 'sixth sense' people talk about. It can be wrong, of course, just as your eyes and ears can be wrong, but your intuition is right often enough that HSPs tend to be visionaries."

Love and Tenderness

HSPs, says Aron, "fall in love harder than others." Bryan Samuels notes, "Steve honors his wife to a degree that approaches worship." HSPs also cry more easily. They are moved to tears by movies, music, and art. Steve can be seen wiping away a tear or two while experiencing musical performances, from Freddie Mercury to *The Lamb of God*. He is also profoundly moved by underdogs, the courage of everyday heroes, the miracle of a strawberry growing out of dirt, and grocery store grand openings. Steve is sensitive, tender, and susceptible to awe.

Think About Thinking

Steve's son Clint recalls many summer evenings, lying on the grass with Steve, looking up at the stars. Sometimes they talked about eternity. Sometimes it got even deeper. Clint says, "I remember him explaining to me how the self doesn't exist. I thought, 'What are you talking about? Dude, I'm nine.'"

HSPs love to think about life and death and how complicated everything is, and they spend more time doing it than non-HSPs. They love to think about thinking. That sounds a lot like the twelve-year old Steve in the shed behind his grandpa's house, the forty-something Steve gazing at the stars with his son, and the current Steve as he meditates in his Zen garden.

Keeping it Simple

"Keep my toys simple and my life uncomplicated." Aron gives this advice to parents of highly sensitive children, speaking from the child's perspective. It's not something an HSP outgrows. Steve's toys are more expensive and go a whole lot faster than a child's toys, but they are still simple. A nice—*really* nice—car is the only toy Steve really wants. And he definitely wants his life uncomplicated.

Steve has a busy mind. If his outside world moves at the same velocity, it is too much. Steve gets frazzled. At such moments, Amy consciously slows her speaking. On a daily basis, she works to keep chaos at bay. Steve practices and advocates slowing down and just being present.

Hary McBride, an HSP, says, "It doesn't take much to make me happy . . . I am capable of being happy all day long just because I saw a parakeet flying in the wind. It's not a 'Hallelujah! My life is complete' kind of happiness, but more of a childish excitement. And who wouldn't want to feel that awe so easily?"

Jason Jaggard experienced Steve's parakeet happiness. During one session, Steve spent a significant amount of time walking Jason through his Zen garden, pointing out all the flowers, plants, and trees. Jason says, "He was like, 'Look at that! Look at this! Look! Look!' It was almost like a five-year old showing a parent. He was modeling wonder and awe and how beautiful the world is. I'll be honest. I was having a lot of judgments come up. This sixty-five-year old man is delighting in a flower and I'm thinking, 'What the hell?'"

Simple, uncomplicated joy.

Low Threshold for Pain

"Amy! I've cut myself. I need help." Amy used to run to Steve. Now she walks. She knows she will probably have a hard time seeing the wound. When she gets to Steve, they both laugh.

"Looks like you need stitches," says Amy. "I'm just not sure where."

HSPs are typically very sensitive to all forms of pain. For Steve, a muscle cramp feels like a vice. A sore throat feels like knives slicing his throat. And a cold—well, get out the will.

Nostalgia

Aron writes, "The deeper processing of subtle details causes you to consider the past or future more." Steve is highly nostalgic. Every visit to Utah includes driving by his childhood home, his grade school, junior high, and high school—with ample narration.

He still remembers his junior high locker combination. He tears up when he hears music he loved as a teenager. Anything that happened pre-1976 has elite status in Steve's mind and memory. It is only with the greatest difficulty that Amy has kept a conversation pit out of their home. They do have shag carpeting.

Physical Sensations

Hary McBride says, "I love the feeling of a soft blanket against my skin. The touch of a loved one has a similar effect. When I walk out the door and the smell of spring hits me, I am instantly in a good mood for the rest of the day." Physical sensations are intense for an HSP.

Steve loves to be touched. It is probably the real reason he loves pedicures. He purrs like a kitten when Amy rubs his arm nightly. He wiggles his arm if she gets distracted and stops. He has toyed with hiring someone to rub his arm all night long so he can sleep deeply. Amy nixed that idea.

Steve loves Arizona in March when the outdoors smells like orange blossoms. He loves cologne and wears it lavishly. Amy notes, "Even when I am swimming my laps, I can smell when Steve walks by, even with my head under the water."

Strong odors, like cooked broccoli, assault his senses and trigger olfactory distress.

Sensitive to Criticism

HSPs tend to react—and overreact—strongly to criticism. They often feel like they are being attacked personally.

Ward Andrews says, "Steve has very few weaknesses, but I think one is that if he is challenged or thinks someone isn't listening to him, he can take it as a personal affront. He feels like he has to justify himself, which he certainly doesn't have to do. I think there's a growth edge there for him, a little bit."

Conclusion

So, what makes Steve Steve? Is it nature? Nurture? Steve's life experiences, the trauma he endured, or the intentional development of his abilities? Is it his personality, energy and intensity, or his high sensitivity?

Yes.

All of these. All of them together.

There is more. There is undoubtedly a wild card, something else we just can't put our finger on.

John Goodie says of Steve, "There are a few people walking this earth who have been blessed with something that is hard to explain." That is the "that" we may never pin down, like the wave upon the sand.

Chapter 33

Magic

In 2009, Steve and Amy took a Caribbean cruise with Paul and Melanie Waite. One evening, they attended a show by Wayne Hoffman. They loved it so much, they attended every show he put on for the rest of the week.

The following is Wayne's experience of meeting Steve, in his own words.

> When I met Steve Hardison, I was performing on cruise ships as a mentalist and an illusionist. The ships held 3,000 passengers, so I met a lot of people. In my profession, it is helpful to profile people. I have come up with seven different categories of people, three main categories and four subsets. Steve did not fall into any of those categories. It was a bit off-putting. I read people for a living, yet I couldn't figure him out. Steve was one of very few people I couldn't get a

take on right away.

I had two interactions with Steve on the ship that really stood out because they weren't normal. I performed several shows during each cruise, so I was pretty high-profile. As I walked around on the ship, passengers often came up and said they loved my show. Steve walked up to me and said, "I've been looking for you." That was a little out there.

"Is this good or bad?" I asked.

He handed me a book and said, "I want to give you this book. This is for you. But I want you to promise me that you'll read it."

"Well, sure. Absolutely." It was a book by Steve Chandler. No one ever gives me physical objects. They'll say a nice compliment, but not give me something. I was perplexed. "Who is this guy? Is this some kind of sales pitch?" Right away, I knew Steve was not like the average person.

My second experience with Steve was after one of my final shows. There was a little hallway next to the stage. It went back into the kitchen area for the staff. No passengers went there unless they were lost. I was finishing packing up in this hallway and Steve walked up to me and said, "All right, I have a challenge for you. If you can tell me my middle name, I will be your biggest fan and I will book you a show in Los Angeles, guaranteed."

"Oh, really?" I said. I love these moments because I have the ability to actually do things that some people—most people—would say are impossible. I said, "Well, I have something for you. I have been carrying this around all day and I didn't know why until right now." I pulled out a folded piece of paper that was in my wallet. As I handed it to Steve,

I asked him what time he was born. He didn't know because he was born in Germany and it wasn't on his German birth certificate. Steve unfolded the piece of paper and saw the words "Forbes 10:10." As you can imagine, he freaked out.

He fulfilled his commitment. He called Ron Hulnick at the University of Santa Monica. They have a big fundraiser each year called "The Night of Magic." They bring in a magician. Steve called him and said, "You need to hire Wayne Hoffman to do your event."

Ron said, "Steve, we already have someone booked. I can't book Wayne."

"Listen, " said Steve. "Pay the other magician whatever he wants. Pay him his fee, but you have to get Wayne. You just have to." He was convincing enough that Ron actually told the other performer to only do half of his set. Ron paid me to perform the second half of the show. It was fantastic. I've been back several times.

It's so hard to explain Steve Hardison. If somebody has never met him, it's nearly impossible. I've never told Steve this, but when I tell people about Steve, I tell them I have given him a moniker: the most intense human I've ever met.

I don't know how he does it, but he creates things. He creates things for himself and for other people. He attracts people. If Steve wanted to wield his powers for evil, he most certainly could. He could start a cult tomorrow. But he uses his power for good. I think he has the ability to do in life what I do on stage. As a mentalist and illusionist, I don't come from "I'm magical. Look at me." Rather, I say to my audience, "I'm magical, and you are too."

That is how Steve lives his life, helping others find their magic. To put it another way, Steve lives his life helping others create a state of being that unlocks miracles (aka magic).

Who would you need to be to find your magic?

Steve, Hunedoara Castle, Romania, 2015

A Note from Steve Hardison

Thank you for taking your time to read this book. I hope that there was something of immense value for you in these pages. Thank you for being wonderful you. Please know that you make a difference. Your life makes a difference. Your "being" impacts your entire world, beginning with yourself and then with everyone you encounter each and every day of your life. It impacts who you choose as friends, what you choose to do for a living, who you marry and how your life will be lived. Remember, being is everything.

Know that I love you. Know that others love you. Know that you are love.

Loving You. Be Blessed. Be you.

SFH/kab

To Alan D. Thompson, the researcher:

As you may recall, on more than one occasion when you invited me to write a book, I declined. You asked me why and I told you that if I ever wrote a book it would be on Being. I also shared with you that if I wrote a book on Being it would not be on Being, it would simply be about Being. I was of the belief that it could not be done.

I let you know that my life was my book and the people who shared time, space, and presence were the chapters in my book. What moved me off that position was your email in April of 2020 wherein you wrote, "Steve, last night God nudged me to write a biography on your life." The rest, as they say, is history. Thank you for your persistence. Thank you for your dedication. Thank you for your efforts. Thank you for the hundreds of interviews you did. Thank you for the hundreds of hours you dedicated to this work. And especially, thank you for your brilliance and your magnificent way of being.

To Amy, the writer:

Amy, it is not very often that one's girlfriend invests over a year of her life to write about her boyfriend. I was and am totally blown away by your commitment and dedication to this and to me. I watched you each day for the duration of this project. I have never witnessed such focus, such tenacity, such creation. And you did this for over a year, six days a week, eight hours (or more) a day. The amazing thing about it is the grace with which you did it all.

As I have often said, you are more talented than any client I have ever sat with. You are more loving than anyone I have ever met. You are a miracle. No wonder when John Patrick Morgan asked his wife if she would like to do a *Be With* session with me, she responded, something like, "To be totally honest, I would rather have a *Be With* session with Amy." I totally understand that.

Thank you for the life you gave to write *The Ultimate Coach*.

A Note from Steve Hardison

Thank you for the life you gave to *create* the Ultimate Coach. I have frequently said, "No Amy Blake Hardison, no Ultimate Coach." You have loved me. You have healed me. And you have created me. I truly am blessed. I love you, my dear, sweet Amy.

The End

Special Acknowledgment

Amy Hardison

To Alan D. Thompson:

Thank you for holding the vision for a book about Steve, his coaching, and his impact in the world, and for patiently waiting until the time was right.

Thank you for sorting through mountains of memorabilia and engaging in hours of conversations with Steve and his family, friends, and clients.

Thank you for your extensive groundwork that is the foundation for *The Ultimate Coach*—without which the book would not exist.

Thank you for your consummate grace in handing me all your research so I could write *The Ultimate Coach*.

Thank you for adding your brilliance to the Being Movement and The Ultimate Events.

Thank you for being our friend.

A Note on the Text

Amy Hardison

While writing *The Ultimate Coach Concentrated*, I came across this quote while reading *Her Last Flight*, by Beatriz Williams: "If you ask me, a biography should read like a novel, not an encyclopedia entry . . . We ought to be able to see the world through our subject's eyes, to live life as our subject lived it, to feel the tick tock of his pulse in our own veins. That's truth."

That is what I have tried to do in the life history section of *Concentrated*. While staying true to the events, the emotions, and the memories, I have created some dialogue to invite you, the reader, into life as Steve and his family lived it.

A very special acknowledgement to someone
who continues to be a light in the world,

Our dear friend, and son of Judy and Erik Thureson,

Jacob "Hella Sketchy" Thureson

"I love you, Jacob! Happy 23rd!"

(January 11, 2024)

~ SFH\kab aka Big Sketchy

References

The source material for Steve Hardison's words, memories, insights, and perspectives are from personal interviews with Amy Hardison and from Amy's personal experience.

Other source material came from the extensive interviews lovingly conducted by Alan D. Thompson. For a full list of sources, please see *The Ultimate Coach.*

Index

Bold numerals indicate pages with photos.

Index

267

(Carroll) 119

U

understanding Steve. *See*
Making Sense of Steve 227-
43
University of Phoenix 159-60
University of Santa Monica
(USM) 211, 247
USM (University of Santa
Monica). *See* University of
Santa Monica

V

Vanzant, Iyanla 96, 102-103,
106, 127, 215
Vehr, John 122, 138-139, 141,
223, 228
Venekamp, Dustin 137
Vernon, Cherryl (Amy's niece)
134-35
visualization 181, 184-85

W

Waite, Melanie (née Dixon)
119, 121, 168, 222, 245
Waite, Paul 46, 121
Walding, Teresa 107, 108
Walter, Jenn 195
Warren, Dr. Lorraine (Rain)
187, 208
We Are All Paralyzed (Sulser)
122
Weber State University 41, 45,
47-54, 55, 56, 75,
Weech, Philip **95**
Williams, LaTrina 215-16
Winder, Parker 195
Woodmansee, Billy 113, 122
working with Steve,
requirements for 167-68

Z

Zen garden, Steve's 240, 241
Zimmerman, Shanti 106, 222-
23

About the Author

Along with *The Ultimate Coach,* Amy Blake Hardison is the author of *How to Feel Great About Being a Mother* (1987) and *Understanding the Symbols, Covenants and Ordinances of the Temple* (2016). She has also participated in five Sperry Symposiums at BYU. Her articles were published in the accompanying volumes.

Amy graduated magna cum laude from Weber State University in 1980 in English. She chose to be a stay-at-home mother, focusing her time and energy on her family. She has been married to Steve Hardison for forty-six years. It has been a wonderful adventure. They have four children and eleven grandchildren.

Throughout her life, Amy has pursued a passion for learning. She also loves to exercise, read, listen to audiobooks, travel, and spend time with her family.

Scan the QR code below to join

The Ultimate Coach Facebook Group

A community for *The Ultimate Coach* to share their
experiences of how the book has impacted them.

www.facebook.com/groups/theultimatecoach

For community, extras and more:

www.theultimatecoachbook.com

To learn more about Steve Hardison:

www.theultimatecoach.com

*Thank you for reading! If you enjoyed this book and would like to
share your thoughts, please feel free to leave a review on
Amazon or a similar site. Book reviews can spread the
word and help readers find great books.*

Printed in Great Britain
by Amazon

41769991R00169